Wounded Hearts

My Roller-Coaster
Journey into
Third-World
Health Care

by Dr. Patience Akinosho

Wounded Hearts

© 2020 by Patience Akinosho

ISBN: 978-1-09835-580-7
ISBN eBook: 978-1-09835-581-4

Disclaimer

While this book is a factual account of the events that took place in the Nigerian health care system, the names of the physicians involved have been changed to protect their identity. Any likeness to an actual name of any physician in Nigeria, living or dead, is purely coincidental.

Dedication

To my mother, Abigail E., and Oluchi, my sister Salome's little treasure!

Blessed of the Lord!

Jesus Christ.

For I am poor and needy;
And my heart is wounded within me.

—Psalm 109:22 (NKJV)

For there is hope for a tree, if it is cut down, that it will sprout again, and that its tender shoots will not cease. Though its root may grow old in the earth, and its stump may die in the ground, yet at the scent of water it will bud, and bring forth branches like a plant.

—Job 14:7–9 (NKJV)

TABLE OF CONTENTS

PREFACE

T HOSE OF US IN THE DIASPORA often cannot wait to travel home to Nigeria; more often than not, it is the only time we truly get to be ourselves. The usual hassles of living abroad are laid to rest during these visits. These trips home, in large part to visit family members in our villages, towns, and cities, at times reflect a celebration of both our personhood as well as our achievements in our new lands.

For a change, the little money we have earned abroad, compared to what's earned through struggle by many of those we've left behind, can be used in many ways to express our love for our people. We are able to help uplift the lives of our family members and those of the community at large. This is why some families pine for their members who cannot return for a visit, even after spending many years abroad.

Of interest is the fact that we are often asked to help resolve a wide range of health problems when we visit home. The difficulty, however, is that the health care system is in disarray and is plagued by both structural and social ills. The result is often high rates of death from preventable and treatable causes. A friend of mine, an obstetrician, cried when she heard her younger sister had died in childbirth, a common occurrence in Nigeria.

Fake drugs also litter the streets. During one of my visits home, one woman who came to ask me for financial help caus-ally mentioned that her family is able to survive because her son, a local chemist, buys drugs, reconstitutes these drugs by adding something else to them, and then resells them at a tidy profit. It was a sincere display on her part of her son's ingenu-ity in helping the family make ends meet on meager resources. Yet, this and other related practices have had disastrous effects on the population's health.

Data from *Lancet Global Health Care Access* notes that Nigeria ranks 142nd out of 195 countries in 2016 in access to health care and quality of health care. As many have observed, issues perpetuating this dire situation include corruption, low health literacy, greed and an increasing desire for quick money, shortage of medical equipment, lack of adequate investment of financial resources, blatant disregard for the lives of the masses by politicians who can easily access the best health care outside Nigeria at a moment's notice, proliferation of fake drugs, predominance of poorly trained health staff, and short-age of health care personnel. (According to the World Health Organization, Nigeria's physician–patient ratio is four doctors per ten thousand patients.)

I bear the scars of someone who was confronted by an unimaginable health problem, one that ultimately claimed the life of my younger sister, Salome. I felt compelled to find solutions for this broken system, which I've come to call Wounded Hearts, after it was laid bare before me as I struggled to obtain a semblance of basic care for my sister. Nonetheless, she was relegated to die in indescribable, unmanaged pain that stripped her of her humanity and what was left of her dignity. At the height of her anguish, her animal-like cries for help could be heard three villages away, paralyzing loved ones who weren't able to help because her body had betrayed her after a botched surgery left her alive but rotting away.

The loss of my little sister, a gentle soul, was a true eye-opener for me into the disaster that is the Nigerian health care system. I would often visit my village, gather the people, recruit local doctors, nurses, and pharmacists, buy large amounts of drugs from local vendors, and set up makeshift clinics in my community for all to receive some level of care. Many have hypertension and can't afford the medication they need to control it. These individuals frequently have conditions including diabetes, stroke, prostate issues, fibroid, vaginal infection (common among young girls), or cervical cancer, and an increasing number of women are dying from breast cancer. While malaria, typhoid, and appendicitis remain the predominant health problems, more chronic disease conditions are taking hold in a society that lacks the sophisticated network of health facilities needed to combat them, but not for lack of financial resources.

Despite the fact Nigeria is teeming with natural resources, it is clear the will of society to invest the required funds is just not there. Nigeria seems ill-equipped to handle the emerging chronic health problems that are fast replacing the above-mentioned triad of ailments. For the affluent, the lack of an adequate health care system poses no grave danger. They can simply hop on a plane and fly to England, South Africa, Germany, India, Dubai, or wherever the next best system of care is. For most of the population, however, the lack of adequate care means unnecessary suffering coupled with high mortality rates from preventable and treatable causes. Is the nation losing its soul? We cry for someone to pay attention.

I don't have the answers for how best to cure the ills of the Nigerian health care system, as there are others better suited to postulate on the issue. I live in the United States. However, I know that the country's elite, by dint of their sheer advocacy power and the magnitude of resources in their control, can help create a health care system comparable to the best in the world. Or at least one that affords its people the opportunity to receive adequate care and a better chance of surviving even the most common surgical procedures.

The wealth of Nigeria belongs to all its people, and its medical community is an integral part of that wealth. There's a need for its citizens to examine their role in the development of the country and lobby the powers that be to establish a state-of-the-art hospital in Nigeria and concurrently advocate for a deeper social consciousness among its doctors and other health professionals. Trained nurses should not be relegated to doing menial work. In more developed countries, they are deemed capable of handling more sophisticated roles, ones that become urgently needed in a society where doctors so freely go on strike, and brain drain to other countries is common. Nurses are essential staff in these other countries, and so they must be in Nigeria. I believe the population should insist on this for its well-being, as well as for the advancement of the medical profession as a whole.

In this book, I attempted to chronicle my journey through the health care system with a sister whom we lost unnecessarily in the process. The care she received was by all standards atrocious, compounded by inadequate follow-up care. If this book encourages one politician or physician to mobilize officials toward a meaningful dialogue on how to improve the delivery of care, it will have succeeded in making a dent in upending the nation's health care system. Nigerians are smart, innovative, and of a generous heart. I believe the day is coming when a Nigerian hospital can receive rave reviews abroad for its pioneering work in many areas of medicine. Its medical school at Ibadan and Lagos has relished accolades in recent years. I believe the availability of and access to a very good health care system remains a doable accomplishment in Nigeria.

CHAPTER ONE

My Unexpectedly Not-So-Great Trip Home

The Commotion

I HAD JUST ARRIVED HOME FOR A visit with my parents, my usual annual or every-other-year journey to Nigeria to see them. The day was uneventful, with lots of family members dropping by to welcome me. Many also assumed that I came once again to undertake my usual health mission, during which local doctors and nurses are hired to provide care, and pharmacists offer free medications to those who are ill. This was an effort that my family and I had begun several years before and that has been much appreciated by the community, a village with more than three hundred families. I also offered these services to a larger population drawn from eleven nearby villages, an initiative cosponsored by a consortium of sons and daughters of these villages, who, like me, resided in the United States.

My sister Salome looked a little pale that evening. While she was never on the big side, she also looked especially gaunt on the day of my arrival. Nonetheless, I was distracted by the kind wishes of our visitors, so it wasn't until late in the evening when I noticed something was terribly wrong with her.

The crowd had gone home, and it was time for dinner. I heard people calling out to Salome. One member of the family said, "Sally!"—as we lovingly called her—"Come and eat." She was a picky eater, so beckoning her to the table wasn't out of the ordinary. As she began eating slowly, my mother emitted a sigh loud enough that I turned to find out what was troubling her. At that moment one of my older sisters, Ra, who was staying with my parents to help out, began pleading with Sally to not throw up her food. Sally stopped eating. Although picky, she normally eats a lot, so this was highly unusual. Suddenly, the room fell silent, and a few people rushed out of their seats. Now I was curious because everyone was focused on my younger sister, but I was momentarily distracted by the children seated around me; they, too, were excited to see me and wanted my attention.

I heard a commotion that drew my attention back to the table. Sally had vomited everything she had just struggled to eat. I jumped to my feet, ran to her, and held her by the shoulder. I asked someone to bring her water. I spoke gently to her, telling her to breathe. She seemed anxious and helpless. I held her tight and reassured her that everything was going to be all right. A few minutes later, all was calm again. Someone reached for a bucket to collect sand from outside to throw on the watery substance on the floor, so the ejected matter could be collected and discarded. They were used to this routine; it happened frequently, and they were all waiting to see if, just this once, the food would stay in Sally's stomach. Alas, it did not happen the way they'd hoped. This had been going on for the past few months, I was told.

I was acutely aware of the tension that took over the room. I sat down next to my mother, who now looked distressed, and gently asked why she was so sad and close to tears. She quietly told me that Sally was throwing up just about everything she ate. This had been going on for three months, and several trips to the local hospital had yielded no noticeable results. I reassured her that I was now around, so things would be different. A few hours later, I asked that Sally be offered light soup so she would have something in her stomach. She slowly took a little bit, just enough, since everyone feared she'd again vomit it out. Tired and in tears, she lay down to rest on the sofa. She apologized for vomiting but said she couldn't help it. A part of her body was working against her, and she was helpless. She wore the expression of someone who had given up, but a glimmer of hope shone through her eyes, as she was happy I was back at home. For the moment.

I monitored Sally for a few more days, to try to determine the cause of the problem and see if changing her diet might make a difference. My mother learned of a recipe for a traditional concoction of herbs, including garlic, which was supposed to curtail vomiting. Sally drank the elixir, which she despised, before every meal for three days after my arrival, but the results were inconsistent. Other remedies sent from abroad by our siblings, Adanne and Kem, had yielded similarly ineffective results.

She could throw up in the morning, skip a day, and then throw up the next evening. In fact, when she would eat, the food would sometimes stay down for hours, and we would be happy that it managed to get into her stomach. However, if anything caused her to throw up, everything would find its way back out, including food she ate hours earlier, looking decayed, almost like fecal matter. I doubted whether the food was even making it into her stomach. In fact, her feces, whenever she had a rare bowel movement, now looked like pebbles.

We began giving Sally glucose and water for energy, mixing up high-protein powders in water to see if it would help. It seemed like the best thing to do, but that, too, would easily be vomited. It was apparently too sweet for her stomach to handle. We were becoming frantic as we mulled the next course of action. So I decided to take her to the local hospital, where she had been seen several times before. I thought that now that I was part of the equation, my presence would produce a difference in the care she received. After all, I had developed a very good relationship with the doctor who owned the village hospital. It was a theory we were ready to test. My hope for adequate care, however, would simply be just that: hope.

CHAPTER TWO

Entering the Nigerian Village Health Care System

The Friendly Neighborhood Hospital

I DECIDED TO TAKE SALLY TO THE local hospital a few blocks from our house early one morning, three days after my arrival in the village. At the hospital, we waited for the doctor, who was busy seeing other patients, to come and attend to us. My other sister who accompanied us, and who knew more about this facility, sat with Sally on a bench located in front of the office where patients typically awaited their turns.

I kept my distance, pacing the pavement outside the hospital. The bench was fully occupied, and I needed the fresh air. The corridor where the bench was located was also outside, which made it easy for patients and their relatives to walk the halls while waiting for the doctor to call them. Most of those who sat on the bench were elderly women and the very ill.

Like me, many who accompanied the sick stood next to the support pillar or walked around to keep busy. A pineapple farm surrounding the building made a pleasant visual distraction. There were other fruits and vegetables on the farm, which the doctor cultivated to help mitigate his food problem. He doubled as a farmer and was known to have a large plantation in his hometown, in another state.

Patients had to pay for what they called a "card" before the doctor would see them. This document has the patient's name and age and permits staff to open a file or medical record for them if they do not already have one. The card also allows staff to pull a patient's existing medical record, which is then placed at the doctor's table for use when the patient presents for care. The patient also has to show their card, which is usually purchased at a minimal cost of 200 Naira (the local currency, about $1.01 in 2015 US dollars), to the billing office to pay for medical consultation fees, any medications prescribed by the doctor during the visit, discharge fees for those who were admitted, and any lab work that was done on-site. As a result, every patient is required to go through the billing office before leaving the hospital.

We paid for the card, and the nurse quickly searched the medical records for Sally's file, which were tucked away in little file cabinets. She pulled out her existing file and took it to the doctor's office. I followed. The nurses were often very nice, and on occasion we would offer small tokens of our appreciation for how well they treated our loved ones. One is not obligated to do so, but it creates a sense that they, too, have assisted in the care process. Further, token gifts and tips from family members augment the meager salaries they are paid.

Unusual Acts of Kindness

The doctor at this facility was a friend of mine. I had visited the hospital several years earlier when I first began contemplating leading locally driven health missions. When I visited his clinic, I noticed that his medical encyclopedia was over twenty-five years old. It was small and worn out, looking like it was printed in the 1960s. I remember thinking, *Wouldn't it be wonderful to replace that manual for him?* It is noteworthy that care at this level seemed grounded in familiarity with the usual complaints of patients he had come to know. Rarely did he have to deal with more complicated cases. The usual diagnoses of wound infections, hepatitis A, dog bites, malaria, typhoid, and appendicitis did not require the delivery of sophisticated care. He knew all the symptoms, and the people knew too well how to describe what ailed them. In fact, one year almost every young person in my village had a surgical scar on their stomach from having an appendectomy.

Of course, today everything can be found online. He also had a computer and a state-of-the-art telephone to look up whatever baffled him medically in the course of treating patients. But that was not the case in those days, about twenty years earlier. I promised the doctor that I would raise money to buy an updated medical encyclopedia for him, and upon my return to the United States that year, I shared the story with a few friends. One of those I told was from the village where the hospital was located, and she took the need to heart. When I visited the doctor the following year, I noticed a freshly minted medical encyclopedia from the United States. He told me that a friend of mine in the US named Ugonma, at my request, had given the new manual to him several months earlier. To this very generous soul, you know who you are, and we say thank you.

I've been to the hospital several times since then, working with the doctor to assist patients from several villages, including mine, who sought care. I always tried to ensure that these individuals did not remain in the hospital long after discharge because of inability to pay their medical bill. Allow me to explain why I felt compelled to do this each time I visited.

It is common practice in hospitals in this part of Nigeria for patients who have been discharged to remain until they can pay their medical bill in full, or fulfill other obligations, even if it meant sleeping on the floor for several days to make room for new patients. There is no other way to collect payment from discharged patients. Patients do not have addresses to which the hospital can send bills, there are no social security numbers that can be used to track or hound them into paying; there are no collection agencies, and no credit scores for patients to worry about and which could inspire them to pay their bills. Hence, the only recourse is to collect the money before care is given, or, for the more conscientious, to treat the patient and then hold them until they are able to pay.

On this particular visit, one young man who had been discharged but could not leave the hospital was still waiting for someone to bail him out. He was about twenty-four years old, from a nearby village, and the only son of his widowed mother. The young man had been hired by a neighbor to climb a palm tree for a few hundred Naira to install a garget, a wine-collecting sack typically placed at the top of a palm tree, with a cut on the trunk to allow sap to flow into the sack. This is something he'd done several times before. On this fateful day, however, there was a vicious snake awaiting his arrival. Being very skilled, he immediately grabbed his knife and launched at the snake, but in doing so he lost his balance and fell from the tree, a long way down. He was found unconscious on the ground with a broken spine.

The young man was kept at home for several days because his mother couldn't afford the cost of medical care. He was also referred to a traditional "bone setter" who was known to help with such problems. After many days of receiving care from this individual, he started to lose leg movement, which panicked his mother. He was her breadwinner, the man of the house. She was able to borrow money from relatives and friends to help pay for his initial medical care, so he was taken to the hospital, where he spent several days in what was considered their special unit. The room held a single bed, and nothing else. Because the hospital was not equipped to handle such injuries, he was treated for several days with antibiotics and pain medication, and then discharged.

At the time of our encounter, the young man had been there for almost a week, two days of which came after his medical discharge as he was unable to pay. I was told during my encounter with the doctor that the only facility that could scan to see what was truly wrong with his spine was in Port Harcourt, a roughly three-hour journey compounded by bad roads. This meant that even if the young man were transferred, anything left of his spine would have succumbed to the potholes along the way.

But here he lay, for lack of funds to pay the hospital bill. He was one of the benefactors of my hospital fund. When I asked him what happened, he narrated his tale—concluding proudly that he killed the snake.

I would stay in touch with the family long after my return to the United States. When he left the hospital, the doctor concluded that he would be totally paralyzed from the waist down or he would die. Months later, the doctor called; he knew how invested I was in the case and wanted to share good news. He saw his former patient riding a bicycle and called out to him. His mother had taken him to another traditional bone setter who managed to piece his damaged spine back together. The young man had survived the unthinkable and made a miracle recovery, and his widowed mother would still have her son to take care of her. The call was unexpected and exhilarating.

This doctor often adopted creative ways to collect payment from patients. Some would come for care and then be sent home right away. But for admitted patients, he would take payment in other ways, frequently in the form of working in his garden for two months.

Sometimes "discharged" patients were displaced from their beds to make room for new arrivals. Some were forced to sleep on a bench or on mats laid on the concrete floor. Desperate to leave, some would lease or sell parts of their land, which sometimes had been in the family for generations, just to settle their medical bills. Nonetheless, the fact that patients at this facility are even treated without upfront payment is commendable. Many other facilities simply send patients elsewhere when they present without the ability to pay.

CHAPTER THREE

The Search Begins for What's Ailing Sally

A Physician Consultation of Hope

THE HEAD NURSE RECOGNIZED ME FROM my previous visits to the hospital to help indigent patients. She went into the doctor's office to let him know I was here. A few minutes later, the doctor called for me to come into his office, which doubled as an examination room. It was a moderate-sized office with little more than a desk and a chair. There was no exam table. Patients simply sat on the chair and told him what ailed them. He had a blood pressure cuff, but I did not notice a stethoscope or any other medical devices that could aid in diagnosis, a source of concern especially, since this facility saw children and infants too.

He was a village doctor, accustomed to hearing people's complaints and discerning what was wrong with them. He also knew from experience that many had no significant problems but simply wanted injections. They loved telling their friends and relatives how many injections they received. It was a conversation-starter, which brought joy to their hearts, and the notion they were so ill that they received injections frequently elicited sympathy.

After small talk about my trip home from the United States, the doctor asked what brought me to the facility. Upon seeing Salome, however, he knew immediately, having seen her there a few times before. He read her chart, noticing nothing out of the ordinary, and then asked her to sit on the chair next to him. He took her blood pressure and said it was normal. He didn't do much else. As he had done many times before, he offered no explanation for her health problem, but this time he filled out a request for a blood test to be done in the nearby city, as his facility did not have the ability to perform that test. He called out to the nurse, wrote a few things on her chart, and asked us to try to bring back the results the next day.

The nurse handed me a bill and instructed me to see the billing staff who would complete the lab order, give us directions to the lab, and take payment for the visit. I did as I was asked, but as we'd be returning to discuss the results with the doctor, I asked her to put the bill on my tab. Because she'd seen me there many times before and knew I was close to the doctor, she agreed.

The Glory of Sally's Birth

We left the hospital and immediately took Sally to the city to get the bloodwork done. We were eager to find out what was wrong with her. Sally was a special young woman, who in many ways was still a child. She was born in Cameroon, where my parents lived at the time, with a form of cerebral palsy; at least that's what one doctor at a hospital in the city would later tell us.

Sally had been a breech birth. My mother told us that the nurse in attendance noticed the position of Sally in the vaginal canal and decided to insert her hands to help in her delivery. There was no doctor in the clinic, and no chance for a Caesarian section (C-section). It was common for mothers to die in childbirth. So this act was to help lower the risk to both mother and child. Indeed, it was not uncommon for a fetus to be manually pulled out to give the mother a chance at survival, when C-section is indicated and no doctor is available to perform it. Of course, in the majority of these cases, maternal and fetal deaths occurred. Many of those mothers who survived the ordeal have dealt with tremendous damage to their reproductive organs and their health in general. Some suffering through gruesome birth experiences even with C-section died, particularly from wounds that would not heal.

In Sally's case, the nurse manually turned the infant upside down to aid her journey through the birth canal. It's a miracle that she survived the ordeal. But that maneuvering led to spinal cord and brain injuries, and though mother and child survived, Sally would have difficulty handling most of life's basic tasks. She was six years old before she began walking, and even then she walked with a slight wobble.

In fact, Sally's legs could not handle a lot of pressure, as they were relatively tiny and somewhat lacking in strength. It seemed her legs were not meant to hold a body that stood upright. So Sally had difficulty walking, and by all accounts, should never have been able to do so at all. But our mother believed in the power of love. So she recruited the children of the neighborhood to come encircle Sally, singing songs of love, clapping their hands, and dancing. Sally looked at all the kids in amazement. These children harmonized, "Sally waker for we, Sally waker for we" (a plea for Sally to walk to acknowledge their diligent efforts), vigorously moving their waists around with such force that it brought enormous joy to Sally's face. She laughed herself into hysteria. It made for an exciting sight, a daily neighborhood concert of sorts.

One of those fateful days, as the children sang, clapped, and danced around her, Sally lifted her butt high up into the air, stretched her tiny legs apart for support, and stood up. The entire neighborhood went into an uproar. A miracle of unmatched proportion was taking place before them.

Let's put this into context: In those days, many people subscribed to ancient belief that children who couldn't walk age-appropriately but crawled on the ground came from the water, so they were not real children and needed to be returned to the water. As a result, many of the neighbors came around to encourage my mother to take Sally to the seashore, place her at the bank and leave her there so that she would go back into the water from which she came. To these individuals, and others who held such beliefs, Sally was thought to be a snake. Since she could not walk like the rest of the neighborhood children, and her legs at the time looked nothing like those of her counterparts, who were now running around and going to school, she needed to be cast away. Indeed, a lesser mother might have listened to these naysayers, who seemed stronger than she was, and might have abandoned her child because she did not fit in.

However, when one of her neighbors said such hurtful things about her Sally, my mother screamed at them at the top of her lungs and forbade them from ever coming around the house again. Then, she went around the neighborhood again, calling on all the children to come and dance for Sally one more time.

But the cry of "one more time" evolved into years. Yet, these children were champions and rallied the troops. These angels among us, God's devoted children, lined up, following each other as they marched to the house to encourage one of their own to walk. One by one, and in little groups, they piled onto the front porch. All the while, Sally's God was watching. So it was no surprise that, on one glorious day, the miracle of patience and confidence in God took hold. Sally walked, to everyone's surprise.

Sally was a gift. In fact, after having seven girls, the last of whom was Sally, my mother went on to bear two sons, one of whom was a menopausal baby. Steeped in her traditional ways, my mother would later say the midwife's turning of Sally had resulted in the repositioning of her womb, allowing her yet-to-be-born boys to find their way out. This was an old wives' tale of sorts.

The Miracle of Love

Sally's ability to walk at age six came through the effort of a mother who believed in the power of the Lord Almighty God, manifested through the love from the neighborhood children. We remained forever grateful to God for the many things that Sally was to us, and the very little she was able to do.

Listen to this: Sally was always able to do the menial housework.

As a member of the household, Sally wasn't immune to household chores such as washing dishes, sweeping the yard, and washing her clothes. She was always able to do these menial tasks; indeed, we considered her a "mamie clean"—one obsessed with cleanliness. But she did them her way. She took an entire day just washing the dishes. She flared up or threw a dish at you if you added one more plate to her pile. Sometimes she just stopped, and Mother had to yell at her to stay on task, if only because she wanted Sally to see herself as a vital part of the family.

Likewise, when Sally swept the compound, you couldn't so much as drop a gum wrapper on the floor, lest she have a fit. But kids being kids, we'd throw things around anyway, just to get her goat.

Sally didn't allow anyone else to wash her dirty clothing. This mamie clean believed no one could ever wash them as clean as she could. However, if no one kept an eye on her while she did her laundry she'd wind up wasting a tremendous amount of the limited water supply to the house. You couldn't get her to stop rinsing her clothes. Assigning chores to Sally was always a production.

Sally also knew how to interact with people. When she finally started to walk, she took off from the house, exploring the entire neighborhood, as if to show her detractors that she equally belonged and that she was as much a child as the other children. It pleased my mother to see her child wander off. I believe that during those walks, Sally appointed herself keeper of the neighborhood. She knew everyone and knew when something was not right with them. She was a friend to the lonely, abandoned, forgotten, old, blind, widow, widower, young, and everyone in between. But her wandering would become a source of fear and concern for my mother as Sally inched toward womanhood.

Unfortunately, Sally did not do well academically because the school system did not have special education teachers; if they had, she'd have fared much better than she did. She attended first grade and stayed there for many years before deciding she'd had enough. Nonetheless, Sally spoke English very well.

Seven girls in all, we were a sisterhood beyond anything you could imagine, with our love for one another imprinted on us by both of our parents. Since our mother was chastised for not having sons, she worked to ensure that her girls were loving toward each other. My father often called us "his foundation." We were terribly loved by this great man, who did not care if he had sons or daughters but was excited that God had found it in Himself to give him children. So we grew up knowing what love felt like through the eyes of parents who loved us unconditionally, as well as from each other.

Here's a case in point. When we were young, we all ate from the same bowl of food. At lunch and dinner, my mother put our food in a large bowl, while she and papa ate from another bowl. When the food was almost gone, regardless of whether or not she was full, our oldest sister, Adanne, left the dining table, allowing the others to eat more. After a few more bites, the second oldest left, allowing the younger ones to eat more. Again, after yet a few more bites, the next oldest left. This continued until Sally alone, as the youngest, was left with the remainder in the bowl. You could cut with a knife the gratitude she felt at that moment. It always amazed her that her sisters were that protective of her, ensuring that she had enough to eat. And Sally really loved to eat. So she would smile, look at the bowl before her, and begin to mutter "thank you sister so-and-so," naming each sister in turn. This was how we did it, prefacing each sibling's name with "sister." Sally may have been toeing the line, but the debt of gratitude was heartfelt. The last to receive a thank you was Coffee, our dog. Sally would yell out, "Thank you, Coffee" and everyone would burst out laughing. Coffee, too, would curl up with his paws on his face wherever he was sitting, which was often nearby as he waited for crumbs, as if to acknowledge the gratitude of a younger sibling.

To compensate for leaving Sally food, our parents also left food on their plate for us. Adanne divided their leftovers among us. But as a show of respect, we each took something out of our own share and gave it back to her. I think we were truly aware that she was being overly generous, leaving very little for herself.

It was this sense of obligation to her younger siblings, ingrained in her early on, that led Adanne to ensure that once she grew up and found work, she'd turn around to ensure each one of us received higher education, even sending us to the United States to further our studies. I sometimes wonder where the love of family has gone in today's society.

Our Sally was delightful, funny, extremely loving, laughter-filled, respectful, and compassionate. No one else can take on her role. She was the heart and soul of who we were as a family, representing the gentler side of us all. She also had eagle eyes, able to see far into the future, and more than once saved our lives because of her ability to do so. She will be missed.

Sally Awaits the Arrival of Her Child

Sally managed to get herself pregnant at age thirty-four, and bore a beautiful baby girl, Oluchi. She was not geographically present to see Sally through her illness. In fact, when it became clear that Sally was going to die, we used the arrival of her daughter to delay her death. We said, "Mamie Sally, Oluchi is on her way. Would you like to see her?" She nodded her head, releasing an infectious laugh. You could see her pain through the hysterical laughter that was becoming all too familiar now. She was used to doing that when she felt anxious, a way of stilling the storm brewing inside of her.

The joy and anticipation of her daughter's arrival was enough to enable her to bear the indescribable pain. Oluchi now lived abroad with a relative, but no one thought to bring her home until it was too late. Her mother's surgical wounds were raw, and she was rotting away now. Sally held on as long as she could, but sadly, her daughter never made it home during her illness. She arrived a few days before the burial. She couldn't recognize her mom when she saw her lying in state. The illness took a tremendous toll on Sally, and at the time of her death, she was an unrecognizable shell of herself.

It's important to reflect a little about the birth of this precious child, Oluchi. I don't know how many families have a "woman-child" like our Sally, who gave birth to a child of her own. While we reflect now on the conditions surrounding Oluchi's birth, we are even more grateful to the Almighty God for her arrival into our family, a gift of unmatched proportion. She will fulfill her destiny.

Oluchi's birth was shrouded in mystery, as she was born naturally, a special grace God afforded Sally. In fact, Sally's pregnancy itself was a complete surprise.

Sally had become a woman in age only. Her mental capacity was challenging. This woman-child would get up in the morning when she lived with our parents and wander the neighborhood aimlessly. You couldn't keep her home because no matter how hard you tried, it would take only a second for her to find a hole in the imprisonment plan, and she would disappear. She'd be gone all day, no one knowing exactly where she'd wandered off to. Remember, when Sally first began to walk at age six, she made a habit of touring the town. It seemed harmless at the time, as walking was a miracle for her, so no one dared stop her when she took off, showing everyone her newfound skill.

But bad habits die hard, and Sally was no longer a child. As noted earlier, the entire town knew her, and you had to wonder how that came to be. It happened because when Sally walked the streets, she talked to everyone she came across. She'd ask how they were doing, taking a special interest in them, and making each and every individual she met feel very special. She asked about their farm, children, husband or wife, chicken, cat, dog, the new dishes they just bought...anything and everything. As a result, she knew everything about everyone.

When she arrived home and our mother asked where she had been, Sally simply smiled, standing a mile away. She was following in the footsteps of her siblings before her. No one dared stand near Mama when they were being questioned. That's because Mama always had a loud voice...and a cane. Luckily, the cane never found a body to land on. We knew better; you simply stood out of range and didn't try to explain yourself. Sally, too, in her own weird way, knew the routine.

Nothing could stop Sally's wandering feet. Upon her return home, she was ready to take flight again. She always lingered near the door for as long as it would take for our mother to forget she was there, and she could bolt out again, forgetting or not caring about any potential punishment. Once Sally found out that those little legs that helped her walk upright, enabling her to join other kids, could take her far around the neighborhood, you couldn't keep her inside. I truly believe that in her small mind, she couldn't stop walking for fear of going lame again.

By nature, Sally was secretive and rarely divulged any information about anything, even if she was sick. So when she disappeared, she was very difficult to locate, and our mother became very worried. Now that she was older, the threat of rape loomed whenever she disappeared. Eventually, our mother decided to send Sally to live with our sister Adanne, who by then lived in the city, in a gated compound with enough space and activity to hold Sally's attention, or so we hoped. Adanne had several house aides who could keep an eye on her, and a gate man who could control—or at least report on—her comings and goings. That gave our mother a sense of security, which would prove to be a false sense.

The Gated House

Who could have thought that what our mother feared happening outdoors, with Sally having access to a large neighborhood that stood wide open before her wandering feet, could happen inside this closed, iron-gated house, with a watchman, no less? We now know that nothing can stop the plan of God. I am reminded of the venerable quote by Sri Ramakrishna, a parable that we heard throughout our childhood, "Man proposes, and God disposes."

Sally was now living behind gated walls, but she still knew everyone in her new neighborhood. After taking care of the daily chores assigned to her for the sole purpose of keeping her busy—sweeping the compound, washing some dishes, for example—Sally would stand behind the locked gate watching passersby on the street. Like I said, I believe she had eagle eyes, and ears, and could tell from their voices or footsteps who was passing the house. So she'd yell out to them, even joining in their conversations. Everyone she called out to responded as though they were old friends. If this happened while Adanne was home, she would angrily yell at Sally to behave, to which she'd politely respond, "I'm sorry, Mommy [her pet name for our eldest sister]. I won't do it again," punctuated by a nervous laugh. However, a few minutes later, vintage Sally would yell out to the next passerby.

Sally continued socializing with people she had no business knowing as if she knew them intimately. How she knew them, no one can truly say. The funny thing was that these people so enjoyed her friendship. Some came by especially to converse with her, and if they saw her standing at the gate, they'd call out to her, so happy they were to see her and share her friendship.

Adanne left Sally home to travel abroad for a month with our parents, as our mother sought treatment in the United States for a nagging eye problem. Upon her return home, without our parents, she discovered a very strange Salome. As was typical, our little sister was not forthcoming with what was bothering her. It was difficult to get any information out of her, even if you threatened her with a cane. Sometimes, she'd take on a deer-in-the-headlights affect. But now Sally seemed to be especially happy. She would either be smiling or laughing alone, going around pushing her belly forward so that it could be noticed. Since there was no other hint than that she was pregnant, as her stomach was still flat, she simply looked strange.

But Sally knew she was pregnant, and in her own way was sending a message to her older sister. Adanne thought she was just very happy to see her back home from her trip outside the country, so thought nothing of it. Sally absolutely loved and was very obedient to Adanne, who had a special way of cuddling her, which was one reason she called her "Mommy." In fact, the special nature of this relationship is why our mother chose to send Sally to Adanne in the first place.

Leading up to our parents' return, Adanne noticed Sally's eating habits had changed as well. Also, she now walked around with a strange smile on her face, as if to say, "Don't you people have eyes to see what is happening inside of me?" I believe each time the fetus moved in her stomach she would react with excitement, and her giggling would draw other people's attention. Yet, she wouldn't verbalize what was going on. Adanne would yell, "Salome, what is the matter with you?" It was a peculiar question to ask, given Sally's bent toward secrecy. Nonetheless, this strange excitement would betray her. Adanne still didn't suspect anything, thinking instead that it was one of Sally's tics.

A November Surprise: The Birth of Oluchi

I accompanied our parents back home to ensure their safe trip, since Adanne had returned home without them a few months earlier. A few days after our arrival, we noticed Sally had gained excessive weight. She was always on the small side. Adanne was reluctant to share her suspicion that Sally was pregnant because she couldn't bring herself to believe it could be true. Nonetheless, a day after our arrival home, my mother suspected her woman-child was expecting. When she asked Sally what was going on, she answered, "Nothing!" then gave her usual anxious laugh. Mama confronted her with her suspicion, however, and

Sally confirmed it by simply rubbing her stomach joyously. The excitement in her face took our mother by surprise, and she was speechless. She stood up, confused as to what to do next, not sure whether to cane Sally or embrace her, and fearing what lay ahead for her.

In most cases, fear should have been the reaction of the day. But that was not the case with Sally. There was nothing our mother could do, so her attitude became one of "there goes the neighborhood." It was futile to try and figure out who the father was, as Sally would never divulge that information. In a strange way, our mother knew this was going to happen; it seemed inevitable. You could never keep Sally locked up in the house, nor could a gated compound curtail her prowess. She had a way of wiggling out of tight corners, and it had paid off for her. There was now a bun in the oven, so to speak. Yet our mother was grateful that it did not happen in her former town when Sally lived at home. Eventually, she let out a strange sigh, as if to say, "Your way, Lord." She took yet another deep breath and sat back in her chair. Though our mother was sanguine about it all, the same was not true of me.

The entire event boggled my mind. I asked Adanne how it could have happened, being as Sally lived in a gated house. Without thinking, I blurted out, "Did she drink it from the tap water in the house?" At that moment, a voice rang out from the other side of the gate, "Salome!" We all looked at each other, wondering who it could be. Sally yelled back a name and laughed loudly. Our mother noted that, as usual, the entire neighborhood liked to talk with her. That person must be looking for someone to validate him today, she thought. Then she said, "Sally is good at making everyone feel special." Nonetheless, Adanne knew her neighborhood as well, and with a little detective work was able to piece everything together. A twist here, a turn there. But she found the culprit. She called the police, but in the end, cooler heads prevailed.

I know that every detective reading this book is now scratching his or her head, trying to solve the mystery. Not to worry; in all things, we give God thanks. A joyous gift would be added to our family, so we were grateful.

It suddenly dawned on me that Sally was now nearly five months pregnant and had not seen a doctor. I jumped into action. The fear of what it meant for her delicate body, vis-à-vis her ability to sustain the weight of a pregnancy, was a little too frightening to imagine.

I initiated a frantic search, and within days I located a gynecologist who had a private practice and was used to caring for high-risk pregnancies. She had a very sophisticated practice. She had studied in Paris and went back every year for continuing education. The cost of prenatal care in her facility was high, but I was getting ready to return to the United States, so I needed to finalize the arrangements. I left Sally in her care, paid for her initial prenatal visits, and prepared for my return home. With the exception of a little pain here and there, Sally's pregnancy was uneventful. She never even had the common occurrence of vomiting. In fact, outside of trying to eat Adanne out of house and home, she was fine. Sally was a very proud mother-to-be, though she knew very little about what it would mean to actually bring a child into the world, let alone care for that child.

Panic during Labor

A little after Sally's ninth month of pregnancy, it was time to deliver. The dreaded signs of her compromised state became evident. Her doctor was not at the facility when Sally was wheeled in with labor pains. She had undergone several hours of pain by herself, before anyone realized she was in labor, and Sally did not know what the severe and strange pain she was feeling meant. Sally began looking strange, and those around her finally noticed that her countenance had changed. Someone asked Sally if she was in pain. She tightened her mouth and muttered something and then began laughing hysterically. At that, everyone around her sprang to their feet. She was asked when her labor pain had started. She couldn't tell how long she had been feeling the weird sensation, so she responded that she didn't know. Now, there was utter panic.

Sally was rushed to the hospital. The nurses tried reaching the doctor, but she could not be found. So the nurses were poised to take on a high-risk delivery on their own, deciding that they would try the doctor again if they ran into a problem, such as the need for a C-section.

To see Sally in labor is to see the miracle of childbirth. As noted earlier, Sally was a naturally secretive and private person. She considered even the act of brushing her teeth a very personal activity. She refused to speak to anyone in the morning until she had brushed her teeth. So she quietly hid herself away to enjoy the pleasure of teeth-brushing. Now, let us put this in the context of childbirth.

The delivery process forces one to expose one's self, without any regard for privacy. We are aware that a woman in labor would have no shame giving birth in the middle of the street with strangers attending her birth, if that became necessary. For Sally, that was not an option. She did not have the capacity to understand that giving birth meant surrendering all of you, including your inhibitions, to strangers. Further, the sensation of pushing is very similar to straining to move your bowels. Salome could not see herself "pooping" in the presence of another human being.

Sally managed to get through prenatal care with the humiliation of having a strange woman probing inside of her and violating her privacy each time. She was not about to let another set of strangers do the same. Unfortunately, no one had actually prepared Sally for the birthing process. That was an unforced error on our part, one that could have been fatal but for the sweet mercies of God.

It was now obvious that Sally was not going to allow strangers to look at her vagina, a requirement for helping with the delivery process. She just did not believe in opening her legs for strangers to monitor her baby's progress. She thought she would get to the hospital and the doctor would simply take the baby out of her (from where, she had not figured out) and give it to her. The prospect of going through the long drawn out process of labor, and obeying commands to push as necessary, was foreign to her.

This was all setting her up for a catastrophe. When told to push, Sally refused to open her legs, facilitating freeing the baby from her womb. She was in pain and the contractions were coming more frequently, yet she continued refusing to spread to allow the nurses to measure the dilation and carry out other required tasks. The nurses were not particularly interested in C-section; it was considered very risky under the circumstances. So they were moved to try natural birth.

Sally paid no attention to the nurses but would push with her legs closed, which can increase the risk of brain damage to the infant or result in death. So my mother was called to assist the nurses. She came in the labor room and began telling Sally to push. Sally would smile at our mom then shake her head impertinently. After much effort without any success, our sister Ra was called in to try, with no additional luck. By the looks on the faces of the nurses, it was obvious that time was running out for both Sally and her baby. It was taking too long for Sally to progress to the next stage. Even if the doctor could be reached, it would be awhile before she could get there given there was no car to bring her, so that was a nonstarter. The head nurse insisted it was best if Sally tried to have the baby naturally, but, she would point out later, she feared they were both going to die. Why she thought that is unclear. However, she had delivered enough babies to understand certain high-risk signs when they emerge, and a few of those signs were now present in Sally's case.

My mother insisted on bringing in Adanne, who was outside on the phone finalizing her travel plans for Paris later that night.

Push! Sally, Push!

It was more than sixteen hours of hard labor now, and very little progress was made. It was a miracle that the baby was still alive in the birth canal. Remember, Sally had been in labor at home for a long time as well without realizing it, let alone informing anyone. So she might have been in labor for more than twenty-four hours, and no progress was being registered.

Adanne arrived in the labor room. She was used to coxing Sally into doing things that needed to be done. She began using language she knew Sally would respond to, the familiar bribery words that brought her much joy. As she spoke in that soft tone, spewing words that Sally needed to hear, she opened her legs ever so slightly, forgetting where she was, then upon realizing would quickly close them again. A nightmare scenario was brewing; time was running out, but as God may have it, the process would continue.

Then, the curtain separating Sally's bed from the one next to it opened slightly. Adanne noticed a relatively young girl behind the curtain, likely a teenager, holding a newborn. Sally lifted up her head and looked in envy. Suddenly, Adanne had a brilliant idea. She changed tact and began telling Sally about the newborn, and how the young girl had pushed her baby out, not wanting her to die in the womb. She then asked Sally if she would like to hold her own baby the same way. She told her that her baby was counting on her, and that she, too, wanted to call her "Mommy."

The joy and anticipation of being called mother overtook Sally, and in that moment, she started pushing for all she was worth. Suddenly, the baby's head could be seen in the vagina. Everybody leaped for joy. But the desire to push further was now met with fatigue. Sally had been there all day and was terribly exhausted. Despite her newfound will to open her legs and push, there was no available energy.

Adanne had to leave soon to catch her flight. She tried encouraging Sally to push one more time, demonstrating what she meant. She said, "Mamie Sally, make as if you have to get a really hard poop out." She told her if she did that, she, too, would be able to take her baby home. Soon, she told the nurses she had to leave, then turned to Sally and said, "Mamie Sally, we can see the head of your baby; she's about to come out." While it really was a great thing for Sally to hear, there was no strength left in her. She couldn't push even if she wanted. She was going in and out of sleep now. What had occurred during Sally's own birth was about to happen again. An evil of fate was trying to repeat itself.

After a few more minutes trying to get Sally to push with no success, our older sister had to leave. The baby was now coming out, yet Sally would try to close her legs to keep the midwives and nurses from seeing her vagina. The baby's head could be seen ever so slightly, but Sally was sapped of strength. The nurses were worried but resisted a C-section.

Adanne was on her way out to her car when she heard a loud shout from behind her. She turned to see one of the nurses, who said in French, "Mama Salome, we can see the baby." The nurse was yelling so loud everyone in the hospital turned. Adanne ran back, forgetting her lateness. When she arrived back in the labor room, she saw that the baby's head was much more visible. The nurses needed the help only she could provide for that one last push.

Adanne began her coaching technique again. Once more there was a contraction, and Sally gave one last push. The baby's head was now fully out, but there was still no more strength to push the rest of the body out. At this point, these very skilled nurses decided to do an episiotomy so they could manually pull out the rest of the baby's body. With one big pull, the baby was out. Pulling out infants was part of the culture of childbirth here. Sally would have to nurse an extremely large cut after her baby was born, and Adanne still cringes when thinking about it, but this was urgently needed to save her baby's life. Sally would hold her own daughter, as her teenage roommate had done several hours earlier.

The entire delivery room staff went into an uproar. It was an unbelievable event. Excitement everywhere! It was sudden, it was unexpected, and the nurses who had taken a liking to this strange and helpless patient screamed for joy at the miracle of a safe delivery. The delivery room staff called Sally *la miraculée*. In a country where maternal and infant deaths were rampant, even under the best of circumstances, Sally and her baby beat the odds. We were indeed grateful to the Almighty God for that favor. Our mother and sister Ra, who had taken turns helping Sally earlier, rushed back into the labor room. "Maman!" Sally muttered, tired and in shock herself.

There would be another time later in our journey through the Nigerian health care system when Sally would call out the word, "Maman," which now seemed to hold a special meaning between mother and child. Sally loved her mother. Sally would always look at her with appreciation for her trusting God and taking care of her as though she had no physical or mental challenges. Our mother would yell at Salome as easily as she would yell at the rest of her children. Ironically, this made Sally feel truly special, as there was no sign of any special treatment. She was simply one of the children, and as such she was subject to the same discipline or love afforded to her siblings.

The Transfer: A New Beginning

Through grace, mother and child thrived under the watchful eyes of our parents, who were now staying with Sally at Adanne's house in the city. Before long, baby Oluchi was enrolled in the kindergarten. Eventually, Maman, as Sally now lovingly called our mother, permanently moved to Nigeria after more than six decades, and since Adanne traveled so much for her job, she decided to send Sally and her daughter to our parents' new home. Maman was very happy to have the company. She would timidly tell us later how much she needed them with her, but was afraid to ask, for fear of being rejected. But to the glory of God, they were on the same page.

Our parents' house in Nigeria had a secure fence and a solid gate. Still, Sally had her time to go out. This time, however, it was just to church for both Sunday services and evening prayer meetings on weekdays. She also joined her prayer meeting's choir group. Sally was a worshipper and dancer for the Lord and participating in these activities made her very happy. She would leave for church a little early, stopping at every door to say hello on the way. As before, everyone in this village got to know Sally. Indeed, she was as popular in Nigeria as she had been in Cameroon. She was loved and cherished by the village folks, who saw her as someone with international flare.

For her part, she began assigning pet names to those who came by the house, with whom she developed unique friend-ships. These names revealed her knowledge of another culture. They became known as *Boo*, *mon amie*, *my combi*, *my brother*, *my mbombo*, and *my friend*. These were normally names denot-ing special ties that she had picked up in Cameroon. Everyone knew their assigned names and would loyally indulge her sense of camaraderie. By this time, our mother no longer feared for Sally the way she had in Cameroon. The concern about another unplanned pregnancy was no longer present. She was home among her own, and a sense of peace now flooded both their lives. God's graces abounded! We could not have known then that in this new, adopted land, we would embark on a journey to save Sally's life, one that would not end as anticipated.

CHAPTER FOUR

The Urgent Need for Answers: False Hope

Is This the Beginning of Real Help for Sally?

S ALLY WAS LIVING HAPPILY IN NIGERIA now. But here we were again in a hospital, about to chart a journey with no clue where and how it would end. Cameroon, which was now just a distant memory, was a place where seeking medical care was familiar territory. Adanne knew all the doctors there and had access to the best hospitals. But this was a new country. We continued our effort to seek adequate care for her, but we now wondered if there was another miracle in sight, and if this system of care held a cure for her. Because of Sally's physical and mental limitations, it was often hard to know what was really wrong with her. She was not always able to articulate what she was feeling or what was going on inside her. This time was no different. We couldn't get her to say how she felt; only when she threw up would we know that something was seriously wrong.

My mother told me that Sally had suffered from heartburn in the past, and that she had been taken to the hospital in Cameroon. The doctor there gave her medication and asked her to stop consuming calabash chalk (*craie* in French), a traditional mud she was used to eating, because it contained bacteria that were causing problems in her stomach. This brownish white mud is especially appealing to pregnant women. But Sally was no longer pregnant; she simply had taken a liking to it. We believe one of her former neighbors introduced her to it during her wandering days, years before. It was unclear if that was what caused her stomach issues. In fact, no one knew where the real problem was inside in her body, only that she couldn't hold anything down.

So here we were in the city, with the paperwork for a lab test in our hand. The local doctor suggested Sally might have hepatitis, a common health problem in the villages. We took her to a three-story building in a city about thirty minutes away. We helped her up the winding, poorly constructed staircase until we got to the top floor, where the lab was located. A young man sat behind a desk in a small office. We sat in the small waiting area for about ten minutes until he called on us and took the lab order. He reviewed it and told us how much it would cost. Like medical treatment, patients had to pay for lab work before it could be performed, so we paid and waited again while he filled out paperwork. We were the only ones there.

A few minutes later, a young woman who overheard our conversation meandered over with a syringe and two vials to collect a sample of Sally's blood. She asked her to stretch her arm right where she was sitting, and then drew the blood. She told us the clerk would be bringing our change shortly, and we handed the change to the woman. She thanked us, and then told us to come back in the morning for the results. Ever so slowly, we navigated Sally back down those awful stairs and returned to our car.

We went back to the village and told our mother about our day's activities. She wore a look of despair, as if she knew nothing was going to come from our efforts to help her daughter. She understood, nevertheless, that we were trying to get to the bottom of the problem. That night was uneventful. We did not feed Sally anything that would cause her to throw up. We gave her hot chocolate and a small piece of bread, which she dipped in the hot chocolate. She went to bed, and all was quiet.

The next morning, we piled into the Nissan truck that my brother Kem in the United States had sent home to our mother. With my sister driving, we set out for the city with Sally and our cousin Ndi, who followed us everywhere as our bodyguard. We waited for the results and, about an hour later, received them. I took a quick look, and her numbers looked normal, with just two outside the normal range. I figured I'd take the blood work back to the clinic and ask for an interpretation, with an eye on those two numbers.

We drove straight to the hospital and dropped off the results with the doctor. He was not too busy at the time, so he glanced at them and said Sally had malaria and typhoid.

It seemed everyone who is sick and goes to the hospital in the village is diagnosed with malaria and/or typhoid. There was nothing seriously wrong, he said, but he could not understand why Sally was having problems keeping food down. He prescribed a few medications and asked us to fill them at the billing office. We thanked him and took the medical records to the billing office, where we paid for the medications and the outstanding bill from the previous day.

We left for home with no clear indication of what Sally's problem was. I said to myself, Sally will die from starvation if nothing is done to help her. I also wondered if her organs would give up since she was not keeping anything down. Moreover, the problem was now approaching four months since its onset. The clock was ticking.

We shared the news with our mother, who was relieved but, like the rest of us, wondered what came next. That night, we fed Sally and tried giving her the prescribed medications. Swallowing was seemingly a problem now. She managed to swallow the prescribed antibiotic for typhoid but couldn't take the malaria pills. She had also eaten something, so we were cautious about forcing her to take anything else lest she throw up. So we abandoned the malaria medication.

That night, Sally did indeed throw up, and with it the medication she had taken earlier. As it had happened before, when hours after she'd managed to keep some food in her stomach till later when she ate or drank something that did not agree with her, she vomited everything again, including the hot chocolate and bread she'd taken in earlier. It seemed like there was a blockage in her upper abdominal area that did not allow for anything to pass through, and an anatomical collection cup was sitting right below her throat. Nothing was getting anywhere. It was like Sally was being tortured. How she had lasted three months without so much as a morsel of food staying in her stomach was baffling to us. But she was losing her stamina and had grown quieter. Adanne sent medication from Paris to assist with her vomiting, but nothing helped.

It was obvious now the light in Sally's eyes was dimming. Our usually bubbly sister was fading away. She often sat quietly alone, apparently in a distant fog, lost in her thoughts. Sally was dying slowly from starvation right before our eyes, and there was not much we could do. Sally was just existing now, for lack of a better word. We were in need of urgent help, but there was no help in sight. As I looked at her, I cried into the air, "God, are you listening? Please help!"

CHAPTER FIVE

Still Looking for Answers

What's Next in This Moment

I RETURNED TO THE HOSPITAL ALONE TO talk to the doctor. I told him what I had observed and noted that there seemed to be a blockage somewhere and that more investigation was needed. I informed him that Sally was now throwing up what looked like fecal matter. He looked perplexed. He reviewed the blood work again and noted that everything looked normal and that if she had cancer of the stomach, the markers would reveal some abnormality. Although comforting, I knew something was still seriously wrong. It is unclear whether the lab that had provided the blood work was sophisticated enough to identify any health problems other than malaria and typhoid. I pressured the doctor to come up with a solution. He wrote a request for an ultrasound of the abdomen to be done in another outside facility. He told us the procedure could only be done at a lab in Owerri, about an hour's drive from my village. It finally looked as though we were moving in the right direction. I was elated but still concerned.

Our Entry Point of Health Care

I looked around the hospital in the village during our consultation visit and noticed that it was a dingy, mediocre facility with few or no resources, and an inadequate operating facility. This was a twenty-three-bed facility, with three moderate-sized wards that each held about three to four patients, a four-bed maternity ward, two private rooms, which housed the more serious cases, and three newly built private rooms for more well-to-do patients. Each had two beds in them. The walls and floors were dirty, the beds were old and rusted and some broken, and the nursing station left much to be desired. The nursing area contained a small table and chair where patients sat to discuss their problems as well as financial situations, and a small area that held a portable screen, where patients received injections.

It occurred to me that even if Sally received a diagnosis of her health problem, this facility did not seem adequate to handle any complicated problem. I hesitated to bring her there should she require surgery. Before I left, I asked the doctor what would happen if surgery was indicated. He informed me that he would have to enlist his friends at the Federal Medical Center (FMC) in the city, a teaching government facility, to come and assist with the surgery. This was a common practice, since he was the only doctor serving several villages. I still was not convinced, for while skilled doctors could be brought to the hospital, the operating facility itself was subpar; it was beyond one's imagination how patients made it out of this operating room alive. We were between a rock and a hard place but decided to take it a step at a time.

The next day, we continued our journey through the maze of the health care system in Nigeria. Arriving in the city, we struggled through traffic to find the lab. We got lost several times until we stopped to ask for directions. Yet, three different people gave us the wrong directions, until a man standing by the roadside not too far from the facility told us how to navigate the "roundabout" to get where we were going. The facility was located in a gated, two-story building on a small street. We made our way inside, where a friendly nurse told us to bring the car inside the gate, as it would be safer there.

We followed the signs and walked up a narrow stairway with uneven stairs. The door at the top opened into a private hospital, one of many of that size in the city. It seemed every doctor endeavored to have a private hospital to make ends meet. We would later learn why that was such a common practice.

It turned out to be a holiday, but the nurses were still on duty. We were the only individuals at the facility, and there were no admitted patients. We asked the nurse at the front desk for the lab technician, but she said because it was a holiday, he was only on call. We were happy to wait rather than drive back to the city and return the next day. It was a treacherous drive, and car accidents, and even kidnappings and carjackings, were common. At that time, relatives were known to arrange the kidnapping of a member of their own family if they thought the victim had money to pay in ransom.

While waiting, I noticed a posting of various specialists on the wall, including a general surgeon, podiatrist, gynecologist, and a few other specialties. I asked whether they had a gastro-enterologist, since we thought Sally might have a stomach-related problem. After checking, the nurse informed us they did, so I was encouraged. I requested a meeting but was told he was a consulting physician and would have to be called in.

The front desk nurse called the physician in charge of the facility, who was at the general hospital, the FMC, where he was on staff, to tell him about us. A few minutes later, her cell phone rang, and she walked with it into another room. When she reemerged she said the head physician asked that we pay 10,000 Naira (about $50 USD) before he could contact the consulting physician. We weren't surprised; as noted earlier, just about every facility here sought payment prior to treatment, since there was no way of collecting after the fact.

Nonetheless, we tried to negotiate the cost of care, but the nurse would not budge. We later learned that 50 percent of the consultation fee (in this case 5,000 Naira) goes to the hospital, and the other 50 percent to the consulting physician. In any case, none of the physicians would see a potential patient without the fee paid up front. We were told all consultants worked for the FMC but moonlighted at private institutions such as this one across the city. Some, of course, also had their own clinics.

Falling Deeper into the Nigerian Health Care System

This private hospital had three patient rooms containing a total of five beds, an operating room, an examination room, a small office, a waiting area that doubled as a reception area, and a small bathroom. Although located on the ground floor, the lab was also part of the hospital. The lab served as point of entry into the system, as it was a source of patient recruitment for the hospital. We, too, would be stepping into the Nigerian health care system through this lab.

I asked to see the operating room to see if Sally's surgery could be done there if it became necessary. The room was bare, with nothing but a surgical table and a container of supplies. The room was poorly equipped, I told the nurse, and that they would not be able to perform a complicated procedure there. We were told later that more often than not, participating physicians used FMC for all their surgeries, although waiting time there for an operating room could be as long as two weeks. Doctors were on rotation for operations there, and they had to wait their turn if they had surgeries to perform on their private patients. Nonetheless, they managed to perform emergency surgery with the limited surgical supplies they did have, as we would see later.

Nevertheless, this private facility was clean, and the nurses were well groomed, friendly, and very polite. In fact, this hospital looked far better than the one in the village where I had taken Sally earlier. The doctor in charge of that facility had done little to upgrade the facility in the twenty years since I learned of its existence. The villagers had not demanded much in the way of appearance or amenities. They were just happy to have a facility to go to. For his part, the doctor noted that because the facility was situated on private land belonging to a family in the village, who had contracted it out to yet another physician prior to his arrival there, he hesitated to renovate or upgrade it because it could be taken away from him at any time. To be fair, the doctor came to the facility as a medical resident about twenty years earlier to do his "Youth Corps" rotation and had simply stayed at the end of his training, taking it over from another doctor. He was the only physician there, although he recruited others from the city when a surgery requiring more sophisticated procedures was needed. It's worth noting that at the time I'm writing this, he is still the only physician there, a very kind and conscientious man. He has now managed to paint the building and tile the floor, not minding if it would be taken from him.

One More Walking Step into the System

Three hours after our arrival in the city, we were still waiting at the private hospital for both the consulting physician and the lab technician to show up. Suddenly, a gentleman wearing a bowler walked into the reception area. Upon sitting down, he took off his hat and noticed that I was looking at his head. He smiled at me and said he was grateful to be alive. He was visiting that day to give financial gifts to the hospital staff. He said he had been shot by an armed robber and could have died had it not been for the doctors at this facility. They had worked feverishly to save his life. There was still an indentation on his head where the bullet was taken out, but he was alive and able to walk on his own. He was forever grateful and wanted to give something back.

Two hours later, another man came through the door. He was tall and thinly built. Unlike the first gentleman, this man walked past us without a word into the room behind the reception area. The nurse followed him, and after a few minutes, she emerged to tell us that the doctor had arrived, and that he was ready to see us.

We entered the consultation room, where the doctor sat waiting for us. He had left whatever else he was engaged in to come see us. Having paid the 10,000 Naira (50 USD), I wanted to be assured he knew what he was doing, so I asked him a few questions. I asked if he was a gastroenterologist, and how long he had been practicing. He hesitated, so I probed a little more. He finally informed us that he was a general surgeon and that he would be able to handle Sally's case because he was one of just a few doctors who did endoscopy in the area, and, he added for good measure, he had operated on more patients than he could count. He also said he was a teaching physician at the FMC. I was disappointed and was tempted to ask for my money back. Maybe I should have, but there seemed to be no alternative at the moment. We had left home more than six hours earlier, and I was tired and hungry. With afternoon traffic, it would take at least two and a half hours to get home, and we'd only have to come back the next day. I just wanted someone to make sense of what was happening to our Sally.

Earlier in the day, before arriving at the private hospital, we had gone to FMC. My older sister indicated it would be a good place to start since we were already in the city. It was the main hospital and saw patients from all over the state. Further, she noted, FMC had more equipment and better doctors. I remembered the doctor at the local hospital in the village telling us that his consulting physicians all came from FMC. So, we thought, why not go there ourselves to see what would happen? Little did we know at the time, it was a holiday, and the doctors wouldn't be around. So when we got there, we were told to just pay for the hospital card and that a nurse would see us. I knew Sally's case needed more than intervention from a nurse, so we left for the lab. Now here we were, no gastroenterologist, and the head doctor was also nowhere to be found.

I allowed the general surgeon to examine Sally. He asked a few questions, took her medical history, placed her on the examining table and palpated her stomach. When he was done, he asked us a few more questions then told us to wait outside. Soon after, he left the room and headed for the door. I followed him past the lobby and asked what the diagnosis was, and why he was leaving without saying a word. My sister would later tell me that doctors in this part of Nigeria rarely tell patients their diagnoses. They simply prescribe medications, and patients buy them, no questions asked. Woe be to a patient if he or she should describe the wrong symptoms to the doctor.

Upon persistent questioning, our doctor explained that Sally needed an endoscopy, noting he would arrange for one, and then he left the building. I didn't get a good sense of what he thought was wrong with her, but we were asked to wait for the doctor who was in charge of the facility to return. He came in soon after, and it was as though they had run into each other on the stairs because the head physician knew exactly what the doctor thought about Sally's case. He stopped and asked if we were okay.

Dr. Eobiped was a pleasant man, in sharp contrast to his consulting physician. I told him the other doctor barely said a word and treated us as though his explanation of Sally's condition would have been too difficult for us to comprehend. He laughed and said he would talk to him about his bedside manners. I didn't take him seriously, but I wanted him to know I needed more information regarding Sally's diagnosis. He reassured us that the general surgeon was a very good doctor and that he would be needed on the case. I asked him why he gave us a general surgeon when we asked for a gastroenterologist. He explained that the one on staff was more than forty miles away in another city and could not come that day because of the holiday. More importantly, he said that if the gastroenterologist consulted on Sally's case, he, too, would have referred her back to this surgeon to perform the surgery, if indicated.

We were now moving deeper into the Nigerian health care system, and a picture of how things were done was starting to emerge. Where this would take us was yet unknown.

CHAPTER SIX

Provision of Medical Care

The Bigger Picture Emerges

T HIS TALL, WELL-BUILT DOCTOR IN CHARGE of the private hospital took me back to the consulting room and told me that Sally may have a blockage, and that surgery might be needed. But first they had to know the location of the problem. As noted earlier, the doctor had ordered endoscopy, but we still needed to do the abdominal ultrasound that had brought us to the hospital and which complemented the endoscopy. We agreed to have both procedures done if they could do them the same evening, so we would not have to return to the city the next day.

The lab technician was running late because of the holiday, of course. However, we paid the fee for the ultrasound and they began to prep Sally for the procedure, and for the endoscopy to come. This meant inserting a tube into Sally's stomach through her nostril to get any fluids out of her stomach. It seemed like a simple procedure; however, I had relatives who underwent these procedures in the United States, and none said they had to suction fluid out of their stomach beforehand. They were told to simply fast for eight hours before the procedure. Sally had not eaten anything for at least twenty-four hours, and her last meal was hot chocolate the night before.

Since the lab technician had still not arrived, Dr. Eobiped decided to go ahead and prep Sally for the endoscopy himself. He called the nurse into Sally's room, where she was now in a bed, and asked her to bring a small tube. He measured the tube down to her navel and then cut a piece to the proper length, handing the rest back to the nurse. He then tried to insert the tube down Sally's right nostril, asking her to swallow as he pushed the tube further down. But Sally could not take the tube. It seemed a difficult process to maneuver, and Sally was starting to cough out blood. The doctor finally told me that he was a podiatrist (in other words, this was not his real specialty), and that he would have to call a colleague, an internist, to insert the tube. The fact that he even attempted the procedure, one he had little experience doing, baffled me. I got the impression he was trying to show off his medical skills, and he failed miserably. We would observe this same behavior elsewhere as we proceeded to seek care for Sally.

So here we were, a podiatrist doing the work of a gastroenterologist or an internist. Fear was starting to overtake me. I was concerned that something bad would happen to Sally. It seemed they were practicing bad medicine, and we had nowhere else to turn. The doctor in the village had no solution, yet here we were facing a health care system that appeared to be in crisis: doctors whose specialties were in one area were performing the roles of others and weren't doing a very good job at it. Normally, this wouldn't be a problem if they knew what they were doing; the doctor in my village is able to perform myriad tasks as the only physician available to a very large patient population who had no other source of medical care. He is, essentially, a jack of all trade, and has mastered many. He wasn't a surgeon, *per se*, but performed many surgeries with the skimpiest of resources. But here in the city, this was not the case.

Finally, the podiatrist stopped trying to insert the tube and called the internist. He explained the problem, and in a reassuring voice the man on the other end of the phone told him he was on his way, and that he'd get the tube in. The lab technician still had still not arrived, so all we could do was wait.

It was now 6:30 p.m., nine hours since we left the village for a "quick ultrasound." An hour later a middle-aged man came into the facility. We'd have to pay another 5,000 Naira (about $25 USD) for this consultation. He was a pleasant man and displayed compassion. He smiled at Sally reassuringly and quickly made her comfortable. It would be a much easier process for him. He figured out quickly that she needed a mild sedative and recommended one. I called a relative in the United States, a pharmacist by training, to get his input on what the internist was recommending. He said it was fine and then spoke briefly with the doctor to chat with him on the dosage. Because my relative knew what he was talking about, the treatment of Sally changed; the doctors were more focused and intentional.

Sally was given the sedative; she soon fell into a deep sleep, and the tube was inserted. There was very little stomach content to suction out. It was nothing more than a foamy secretion, barely enough to warrant the production of placing the tube in her stomach. I thought, *What if the blockage was so bad that they had perforated her stomach trying to get the tube through?*

The internist left quickly after inserting the tube. An hour in, with nothing more coming out of Sally's stomach, the lab technician arrived. I should point out here that this individual was the only person responsible for performing almost all the procedures that the facility offered. Whatever you needed, he'd be doing it. They were now trying to wake Sally up but couldn't rouse her. The technician waited around for about twenty minutes and then decided to leave. We had waited more than eight hours for him, but to him, twenty minutes was an eternity. In the blink of an eye, he was gone. I felt like crying.

Nothing was falling into place. I missed a giant clue that we had entered the wrong health care system. Our zeal to get help for Sally was coloring our logical thinking. There were obvious signs of danger, but our exhausted minds were overwhelmed by the dread of the long trip back and forth from the village, the urgency to get Sally help, and the realization that time was running out. At that point, it seemed any help was better than no help. That was an egregious error on our part. Reflecting back on these things now, hindsight being twenty-twenty, I really believe we dropped the ball. We were supposedly in the hands of the best that society could offer. But the best was not nearly good enough.

Next Round in the Care Process

Sally finally woke up and was dressed so she could be driven to the site of the endoscopy. With the tube still hanging down her nostril, we left, disappointed that we would still have to return the following day for the ultrasound. It was now 8:00 p.m., nearly twelve hours since we left the village.

We kept in close contact with our mother throughout our stay in the city, giving her an hour-by-hour breakdown of what we were experiencing. She was reluctant to have Sally undergo any further procedures. She felt her body, now weak from starvation, could not handle any additional medical probing. She was also afraid that they might recommend emergency surgery and was not ready to deal with that possibility. Our specific goal was an ultrasound, and since that was noninvasive, she had approved our trip to the city to have it done. Now that Sally was being sedated and tubes passed through her nostril, and the procedure would have to be repeated when endoscopy was done, it was a little too much for Mama to swallow. If something were to go wrong, she feared she would not be there on time to help or to say goodbye. But we convinced her that everything we were doing was necessary, as there was no other way to find out what was wrong with her special daughter, or treat it, whatever it might be.

The general surgeon who consulted on Sally's case earlier owned one of the few facilities in the city that did endoscopy. The podiatrist took pity on us and offered to lead us to the endoscopy site. We followed him through traffic to a facility about thirty minutes away. It was 8:35 p.m. when we arrived. I believe Dr. Eobiped had spoken to him as he had promised because now the general surgeon was more polite and engaging and asked many questions about Sally's case. Then he told us the procedure would cost 35,000 Naira, 10,000 more than we were told at the private hospital.

We registered Sally and paid the fee (about $176 USD). We were told to bring six gallon-size bottles of water. It was unclear what they needed the water for, but we would later learn it was necessary for the procedure. Because we arrived late and did not know about this requirement ahead of time, he told us to bring them the next day. The general surgeon also arranged accommodations for us, learning from his colleague of our circumstances.

Sally was dressed in a hospital gown and taken into another room, the tube hanging out of her nostril now attached to a collection bag that dangled at the other end. A few minutes later, the nurse walked into the small waiting area and beckoned me to follow her. She had paper slippers in her hand and asked me to take off my shoes and put them on. I did as she asked, then followed rapidly behind her. This time, she took me back through the outside door to the facility, then to another side door. I noticed that this was the physician's private home, but he had converted a portion of the house into a medical facility.

As I walked into another small attachment to the house, I realized the doctor was inviting me to observe the procedure. I was a bit frightened but at the same time curious. I was afraid Sally might die during the process and didn't want to witness that. Yet, if that was to be her fate, I did not want her to die alone. Further, I had given them the impression that I was a strong and forceful advocate, someone who was familiar with what proper medical care looked like and knew that what we were being offered did not measure up. Sally was so fragile now, and undergoing another invasive procedure was a frightening thought. But we needed to keep an eye on the doctors. I found myself in a bind of my own making but reluctantly accepted his offer to observe.

He began the procedure when I came into the room. The podiatrist was also in attendance to observe. With his botched attempt to insert Sally's stomach tube fresh in mind, I truly hoped he wouldn't think this would be sufficient training for him to want to try to replicate the procedure at his facility.

By the time I entered the room the doctor had removed the old tube in Sally's nostril and inserted another one through Sally's mouth. The doctor pumped gallons of water through the tube and inserted a smaller tube that held the scope. I was told the water helped clear the path so the doctor could see more clearly on the monitor.

He used at least four bottles of water during my stay. He struggled for a long time; the scope moved erratically and could not pass beyond a certain point. He stopped the procedure and informed us he needed to do a CAT scan of the abdomen, as there seemed to be a blockage. Again it occurred to me that if there was a blockage, there could have easily been a perforation, as the doctor struggled for a long time to pass through before abandoning the effort.

My mind was now a mixed bag of what-ifs. I was somewhat relieved when the procedure ended. Sally was still alive, and I was happy about that. I waited for a while to see if there would be any adverse reactions to the procedure, but there were none. Sally was asked to sit on the table to catch her breath and then told she could go back to the waiting area. It was nearly time to leave the facility. She still had some strength in her because she had been given an IV drip at the previous facility, but our Sally was now quiet and distant. She was slowly fading away.

A Night on the Hospital Floor

It was now 10:00 p.m. We knew at that point that we could not return to the village that night, although only one hour away. We told our mother we had to spend the night in the city, and she agreed that at that time of night it would be suicidal to begin a trip home. As mentioned earlier, Nigeria has a problem with armed robbers, carjackers, and motor accidents. It was also obvious that Sally needed to be monitored during the night. So much had been done to her, and we wanted to be sure that she was all right. We also knew we would have to do the abdominal ultrasound early the next morning. We let our mother talk to her.

We had not given any thought to a hotel stay because this was a medical visit, not a vacation. Besides, we did not trust the hotels to be safe for night travelers. We spoke to the podiatrist, and he offered us a solution. It wouldn't be free, but it would be safer for all concerned. He advised us to spend the night at his private hospital, where Sally was seen earlier. For 8,000 Naira (about 40 USD), Sally could have her own room, and we could sleep on a mattress on the floor. She would also be put on an IV to replace any fluids she might have lost during the endoscopy process. Further, a doctor would be able to examine her in the morning to ensure she was all right. We agreed to this arrangement.

On our way to the hospital, we stopped at a restaurant to buy dinner. We had not eaten all day, so we were famished. We got takeout at one of the restaurants and ate in the car. We did not give any food to Sally. She was still tired from all the procedures and still loopy from the sedative. We chowed down on a somewhat decent meal and then continued on to the hospital. Later in our journey through the health care system, I would become very sick from eating food from local restaurants.

The nurses at the hospital were happy to see us. They had taken a liking to Sally, a gentle soul who was trying to deal with a very difficult situation. A new nurse had also joined the group that we met earlier. She had been informed about Sally and was eager to meet her. We were treated like royalty.

They gave us a room and placed Sally on the bed, an IV inserted into her left hand. It was now 11:30 p.m., and the nurse put a mattress on the floor for my sister and me, and then wiped it down with alcohol. She put a sheet on it and handed us two pillows. We kept a close eye on Sally. Ndi, our cousin who accompanied us, rested on an empty chair in the reception area, as there were no other patients. We eventually closed our eyes and hoped for a quiet, uneventful night.

CHAPTER SEVEN

A New Road to Travel on the Journey to Health

Another New Face in the Puzzle

THE NEXT MORNING, A VERY NICE female doctor came in the room to examine Sally. She had a very accommodating personality and was genuinely concerned about our sister, particularly after noticing she was a very special woman-child. Dr. Walters went over her history and noted that Sally was starting to pass what she called "starvation stool." There wasn't much in her stomach, so she could barely use the toilet. And when she did, she passed pea-shaped feces. The doctor was very concerned and thought it best to hurry up and find out what was wrong with her. We told her we had been advised to get an abdominal CAT scan. She was not sure there was a need for it, since the endoscopy had found a blockage, and thought they could proceed with surgery based on that finding. But we were determined to get the scan to complement whatever the endoscopy revealed.

Dr. Walters (not her real name) was also a consultant at the private hospital. She was one of the specialists whose name I'd seen on the board earlier. She also advised us to get a gynecologist to examine Sally. We agreed, and one was called in. We were now on the hook financially for this consulting doctor, the gynecologist, and all the services that Sally received the day before. We were not prepared for the cost, but we made arrangements to return to the facility to pay what we owed.

That morning, Sally had the ultrasound downstairs in the lab, but it was a waste of money because it revealed nothing. They couldn't make out the images, either as a result of the technician or the machine itself, which appeared old. By now, we were in direct contact with the facility that would perform the abdominal CAT scan, so after the consultation with Dr. Walters, we headed home. We needed to regroup, fill in our mother about our journey, and decide on the next course of action after spending twenty-four hours—much of it unplanned—on the road.

The Man from London

On our way back home that morning, we called the CAT scan facility, one of just two in the area, which could provide the service. One was about an hour away in another city, and the other happened to be in the city where Sally was being seen by a collection of doctors. We decided it was best to stick with the latter facility and not begin a new journey into an unknown health care system. We also figured that since Sally's doctors would be closer to the facility, they could get the results much sooner.

The owner answered the phone with a slight accent. I asked him where he was from, and he said he lived in England, and that he comes to Nigeria once a month to oversee the lab. "It's still a work in progress," he said. Then he noted he needed his income working in England as a radiologist to help fully furnish the facility. He had an ambitious plan for it, which we would observe later.

I told him what we needed, and he gave us an appointment for the next day. The procedure, we were told, would cost 45,000 Naira (about $225 USD), though we were charged a little more when we arrived the next day. We were trying very hard to move things along. Sally needed resolution to her problem, and it was rapidly becoming an emergency. She was still throwing up. But since she had an IV in during her short stay at that hospital, there was no urgency to feed her. Indeed, by now she was afraid of food. We knew we were running out of time.

We got home and briefed our mother about our journey. She, too, was eager to get answers. I spent an hour with Mama and Sally to make sure Sally would be okay. Since she hadn't ingested anything but liquids, she did not throw up. I went off to my room to rest. Thankfully, Sally had a peaceful night. The next morning sister Ra, Ndi, and I arrived at about 8:30 a.m. for the CAT scan. We were thirty minutes early; in our zeal to be the first ones there, we left very early for the hour drive to the site. A security guard told us to park outside, close to the gate, and wait for the staff. About twenty minutes later, they began to arrive, passing us at the gate. We waited a few minutes more outside before we were allowed to enter the compound.

At exactly 9:00 a.m., the staff emerged from their offices and huddled in prayer before commencing the day's activities. About four of them sang songs of praise, clapped their hands, gave thanks to God, and then dispersed. It was a comforting sight. The owner later told me that nothing happens in the facility without morning prayers.

We noticed an X-ray room, mammography area, and several other scanning rooms. It seemed well-equipped, and many other machines were waiting to be set up. The owner planned for this to be a state-of-the-art facility, and it appeared he was well on his way toward achieving that goal. He later informed me he'd bought the machines in the United States, and they were each at least five years old. He said that although he lived in England, he had the ability to read scans via the Internet so didn't always have to be onsite. This all sounded good, but I did not feel confident there were enough technicians to operate the various machines.

The Very Dangerous Technician: A Nurse Wannabe

At this facility, Sally was given a concoction to drink. Because it was a liquid, she was able to swallow it. Although the owner knew of our dilemma and made the concoction very light so it would pass through to Sally's stomach, sister Ra had to be creative to get her to drink it all. Then she was prepped for bloodwork.

We were put in a small room. One of the two staffers began trying to insert a needle into a vein on her right hand. He struggled for a while, saying "her veins are too strong," but he continued to try. At that point, a second nurse in a blue uniform stepped in to help. In a few seconds, he was able to draw the blood. Later, he told me that the first person was not a nurse, but he always tried to draw blood, because he'd seen the nurses do it enough times and thought he could too. *He could have punctured a vein*, I thought. I was curious why the second nurse hadn't said anything to his colleague or their boss, and why he allowed him to tamper with people's lives. I was reminded of the podiatrist who earlier stepped outside of his specialty when he tried inserting the tube to drain Sally's stomach, which also could have caused terrible harm.

We were asked to go back to the reception area and wait awhile as the room was prepared for scanning. At that moment, the owner came to offer a tour of the facility. I had a slight American accent, one gained from living abroad for many years, so he knew I was a stranger to the country and that he needed to pay special attention to me. Also, he had taken a liking to me when we spoke the day before.

During the tour, he told me a little about himself and his ambitious plans for the facility and the community at large. He was providing a much-needed service where such technology was scarce. The only other facility like this one was in a city more than an hour away, and it was run by experts from India.

He noted that it was time Nigerians invested in Nigeria, and there should be no need to travel to Europe or India for simple procedures that could be done in-country. He noted that equipment such as that in his facility should be available to all for diagnostic purposes.

We were soon called into another room, and there he was again, the wannabe nurse who had unsuccessfully tried to draw Sally's blood. We were told he was the scan technician. He seemed to know what he was doing in this instance, and the doctor watched on a screen from a small room. I watched through a clear glass door in the waiting area. The scan was done in a relatively short time, and Sally was asked to get dressed and wait in an adjacent room, where the radiologist was monitoring the procedure. Soon, the radiologist came into the waiting area and, knowing by now that I was from the United States and was no shrinking violet, asked me to come and look at the screen.

I leaned on a chair next to him. Apparently, there was a blockage. He noted that the lining of Sally's concentric pyloric had thickened to 15 mm, when the normal gastric wall thickness should be somewhere around 4.5 mm. He diagnosed gastric outlet obstruction as a result of severe pyloric stenosis. He also observed a 16.9 × 13.6 mm enlarged lymph node at the porta hepatis. At the time, I did not understand his conclusion. He withheld the fact that he suspected gastric cancer. He insisted he would forward the completed report to the doctor, but there was an obvious blockage. At that moment, we knew conclusively that Sally required surgery.

We waited while the doctor wrote his report. We left that day with a copy of the results and a CD containing the complete findings. He would later email the results to the consulting physician who had referred us.

We went home and watched Sally carefully. In the middle of the night, she awoke in panic. She couldn't breathe properly, as she was weak, and looked terribly emaciated. She had not ingested anything but a few sips of glucose water in days. I stayed with her and my mother in their bedroom until she fell back to sleep. I returned in the morning, and Mama told me it had been a rough night. Sally had spoken to her in a manner that indicated she was giving up, that she knew she was dying. She had said, "Mama, na go this" ("Mother, this is goodbye. I am leaving").

That day, I decided to rush her back to the Federal Medical Center. I had developed a good friendship with the two doctors, the podiatrist and the general surgeon, Dr. Agamop, who were both on staff. More importantly, I thought Sally needed emergency intervention, and Dr. Eobiped was one of the chiefs in the emergency room. I called from the house and told him we were leaving the village for the FMC and asked him to meet us there. I figured he would be able to move us through the emergency care system, and I was right.

In hindsight, as events unfolded in this disjointed health care system, perhaps that trip to the hospital was ill-advised. A silent cry for help seen in the face of an emaciated woman-child would soon become screams of horror too hard to forget. The journey that day was the beginning of the road to hell.

CHAPTER EIGHT

The Trip to the Emergency Department

Up and Running

THAT MORNING, I GOT READY AND left with sister Ra and Ndi for the FMC. We had the results of the scan and needed to take them to town, where we could count on electricity, so sister Ra could use her iPad and scan the document. Our plan was to email the results to our relatives in the United States, who would be well-positioned to help explain the findings. We had not read them, merely accepting them in an envelope. Perhaps we were too scared to know what was in it.

We arrived at the emergency room at about 10 a.m. It was crowded, nurses filling the room. There were two resident doctors. There were about eighteen beds in an open space without any dividers, a desk that accommodated about eight nurses and doctors, and a small room that held supplies and a triage bed. There was also one bathroom, which everyone shared. We observed that water had to be carried from outside into the bathroom, for flushing.

We waited outside for Dr. Eobiped to arrive, as there was some commotion in the room. Sally at this time didn't seem to require emergency care, and when he arrived, he asked why we'd brought her to the ER. She was neither bleeding nor unconscious, criteria for an ER visit. She did not look like she was dying. I told him about her rough night and that her present appearance was a stark contrast from hours before. He understood and said since we were there now, it was best to get her through the system to see what could be done for her. He called out to one of the residents in the emergency room to triage Sally outside, as there was no space inside. The doctor said he'd return to check on us. The resident, a pleasant young man, took Sally's vitals. Her blood pressure was somewhat low. Since there was no bed on that floor, he asked us to wait outside and said he'd come for us as soon as a bed became available. We found an empty chair, and Sally sat down in it.

The outside area was also crowded with family members waiting on news about their loved ones or the chance to go in to see them. A security guard manned the door, helping to keep people out. Sister Ra used this time to scan the results on her iPad for transmission to our relatives overseas. They included a nurse practitioner, a Master's-prepared nurse with more than fifteen years of clinical experience, and a pharmacist. We would later realize that the doctor had not included his conclusions on the report; rather, he'd given his colleagues a different report from what he gave us.

We had difficulty sending the email from the FMC, but our efforts kept us busy during the long wait. We finally succeeded and waited for feedback. We wanted a consensus on what they thought the problem might be and additional insight from their physician colleagues in the States.

We had nothing to do after sending the document except continue waiting. We became increasingly aware of the gravity of the situation facing us. As I write this, I now recognize that as we ran around looking for help for Sally, she had grown disturbingly quiet. She knew what the rest of us didn't know at the time: that she was dying. She was entering her fourth month of not truly eating anything. How her body had withstood that pressure of starvation was beyond me, other than her desire to live and her hope for being saved. After all, her beloved big sister from America was here now.

Sally had a tendency of looking at me and releasing a sudden laugh that would always draw the attention of anyone nearby. Understanding that it was her way of showing love and acknowledging that she was happy that I was around, I would usually say, "What is it, Mamie Sally?" And in her usual way, she'd shake her head in joy that she was with her big sister, and then say, with a gigantic laugh, "Nothing." But that was no longer there.

A Place for Sally

There was still no space in the emergency room, so Sally was put in the supply room after about four hours waiting outside with what was considered low blood pressure. I did not feel stressed out about the wait, because I knew that even in the United States, it was not uncommon to wait up to fourteen hours at the emergency room, particularly in academic or teaching hospitals, and we were far below that threshold. We were told she'd be moved within an hour to the main floor of the emergency room, whenever a bed was available.

One woman who had been discharged was sitting on a bed near the door. For all intents and purposes, Sally was to take that bed. The woman had been discharged and was expected to leave the ER within the hour. But six hours later she was still there, and Sally was still on the bed in the supply room. Upon inquiring, we learned that the woman had received a blood transfusion, and that the blood bank was waiting for her relatives to come and donate replacement blood before she could leave. In the end, that patient did not leave that day, as it took twenty-four hours for her to rally relatives for blood donation, so Sally had to wait for another bed.

Patients came and went, victims of accidents (adults and children) and those with all sorts of ailments. The guard was not always successful keeping families out of the emergency room as they rushed in to see their loved ones. Indeed, like many of the families, sister Ra and I would not leave Sally's bedside, even while she was still in the supply room. I would later befriend one of the guards, and he would locate a chair for me to sit on near Sally's bed when she was finally moved to the main floor.

Still in the supply closet, Sally was given an IV and had an adverse reaction. She began hallucinating. I am not sure if it was pure saline solution or if there was medication in the mixture, but when a nurse decided to take out the IV bag, Sally immediately felt better and was smiling again.

My friend Dr. Eobiped occasionally came to see us in the ER, though he had rounds to make. He reassured us that Sally would be given a bed in the surgical ward within a few hours, and that everything would be all right. He also reached out to Dr. Agamop, who had consulted with Sally, asking him to come and visit her in the ER. He would not come to see us until the next day; it was clearly not enough of an emergency for him to come to the hospital that day.

When we arrived, it became clear that the facility had no equipment to handle any sophisticated health problems. The doctors were working with bare hands. There was not even a defibrillator in sight. In fact, three individuals who arrived after we got there were in dire condition, and one woman who was in a coma when we arrived was judged to be in critical condition. The three appeared to have difficulty breathing, but neither a ventilator nor any aggressive measures were put into effect to help them, and they died soon after we arrived. The comatose woman died the next day. Their bodies were left in place for a while before being moved. It remains a mystery to me how critically ill patients survive in that system of care.

I promised myself that when I returned to the United States, I would do whatever I could to send at least one defibrillator to the emergency room of this hospital. In fact, one of the residents asked if I would help because he thought it was such a vital piece of equipment, and he didn't think the government would ever purchase one. It's worth mentioning again that Nigeria is a rich country and the cost of a quality defibrillator—less than $2,000—wouldn't bankrupt the government. The absence of one was not for lack of money but a result of misplaced priority and greed. The doctors noted that the government was known to divert funds allocated for the population's health to more personal use. Here, back in the United States, I'm still working on getting a defibrillator for the hospital. But the doctors who asked for it have since moved on.

We waited with Sally in the emergency room for two days before a bed became available. Again, lengthy waits in the ER before being moved to a floor are not uncommon in the United States, so we were patient. The problem was that the area was overcrowded, not only with patients and their relatives, but with medical staff who had to maneuver in very tight spaces to do their work.

Dr. Eobiped finally used his authority to move us from the emergency room, where we might have lingered for a third day had he not found a bed in the pediatric ward. Because Sally was slated for surgery, she'd eventually have to be moved to the surgical ward, but a room was not yet available there. We were happy just to get this temporary room; the ER environment was not conducive for long stays.

It's worth noting the dedication of our nurses during our time in the ER. They were efficient, frequently working with their bare hands to save the lives of people on the brink of death. You had to wonder what could have occurred had they been given the proper equipment to care for critically ill patients.

A shout out, too, to the residents who filled the emergency room, each beaming with pride at the prospect of one day becoming a full-fledged doctor. They were young and green, but what they lacked in experience they made up for in enthusiasm.

Nigeria, you owe your doctors and nurses a true commitment to improve access to resources essential for the delivery of care. To ask them to work with no equipment is unconscionable when they hold the lives of your citizens in their hands. You are also putting the lives of these young people in jeopardy. You need to upgrade even the simplest resources. Some doctors are using torn little medical encyclopedias that were issued in the 1960s or '70s. We remain hopeful that with the advent of the internet, Google, smart phones, and more, your medical professionals will soon have much better access to a wide range of vital medical information.

CHAPTER NINE

Leaving the Emergency Room for the Pediatric Ward

Adults in the Pediatric Ward

YOU HAD TO PAY FOR EVERYTHING upfront before you could be treated, be it a bed in the ward, medication, or what have you. We paid 50,000 Naira (about $251 USD) to guarantee a spot in the ward, and that afternoon, we were transferred to one within the pediatric unit. Sally was placed next to a woman who had just had a mastectomy and who also could not be accommodated in the surgical ward. She was a pleasant woman of about sixty, and her presence made things bearable. She told us where to fetch water for the morning bath, where to get hot water for tea, which vendors sold the best food in front of the hospital, and shared with us some tidbits about the nurses, like which ones were friendly and helpful. She owed her insights to being there for a week. We were grateful for her wisdom and that we were not the only adults in the pediatric unit. We would be joined later by two other women.

We unpacked our things and wondered what would happen next. We were hoping the consulting physician would come to see us to let us know when surgery would be planned. We waited all evening, and he did not come but sent two residents. They seemed to be new in their roles, perhaps first-year residents. One, a female about twenty-three years old, made small talk with the other physicians, who were busy working on patients. Then, she talked on her phone while the other, a male, attempted to set up an IV for Sally. She checked Sally's vitals and gave her medication, but she seemed uninterested in caring for her patients and never acknowledged the rest of us.

Often after that first encounter, she came alone. We never had an opportunity to talk to her about Sally's situation or share our observations, because she was always on her phone and always acted detached from her work. Eventually, we found a more seasoned resident, a God-fearing young woman who took a liking to Sally and went out of her way to help us. Other residents also came to Sally's bedside late at night to take her information, adjust her IV, or prescribe other medications. Those who were more advanced in their residencies tended to chat a little with us, while the younger ones were more aloof, or, like the cell phone talker, detached from what they were doing.

Dr. Eobiped came by that first evening to check on us and reassure us that the consulting physician, Dr. Agamop, would be coming to see us the next day. He, too, was concerned about the carelessness of this physician, but we had no choice. Everyone I asked told me he was a good surgeon. He was one of two doctors, who had a huge following of residents, and his team trusted him; either that, or they did not want to say anything bad about him.

The evening we arrived in the pediatric ward, the physician to Sally's roommate brought his residents with him to see his patient, whom we now knew as Mamie Dorothy. He was friendly and talked to the elderly woman as though they were friends. He spoke reassuringly, as she asked question after questions about her treatment, her bandaged wound, and the removal of the suction sac that collected bloody fluid from the affected breast. He was pleasant, and I wanted him to be our doctor but was told it was too late to change doctors.

It was now day three at this hospital. During our lengthy stint in the emergency room, we slept on benches arranged in a nearby area for clinic patients. It had a fan, which meant fewer mosquito bites if you were among the early birds who claimed one. Mosquitoes were a constant reminder of life in Africa, and we were beaten down by them. I was on malaria prophylactics, so I wasn't unduly concerned.

Informal Ties and Hospital Care

Many of the menial jobs required for hospitalized patients are performed by family members or friends who accompany them. You fetch water for toilet flushing, provide clean bowls for meals, donate blood, shuttle blood vials to the lab, travel to local pharmacies to purchase medications that were unavailable in the hospital, obtain hot water for bathing or tea, and much more. Mamie Dorothy had no children, so she was accompanied by her nephew, a boy of about twelve. He handled all these tasks, bought food from street vendors, and performed other functions. Those accompanying patients also were responsible for gathering supplies for wound care and paying the bills before their loved ones could receive services.

A patient who is vulnerable is unlikely to be able to handle these little but very important tasks. Without a formal or informal support system, the patient would be neglected and would not receive appropriate care. Indeed, one of my cousin Ndi's main roles was to fill prescriptions as the doctors wrote them and take blood to the lab for testing.

Settling In

Sally grew stronger upon leaving the emergency room. She ate fresh fruits like oranges and papayas and loved them. She did not throw up and seemed to be adjusting well. In fact, she carried on conversations with her roommate as though nothing was wrong. We were elated by her progress; she looked strong, so we were hopeful that her body would be able to handle the surgery. Nonetheless, we felt the need to again stay with our sister to make sure she received the care she deserved, so there'd be no going home for the time being. Also, as noted earlier, the journey could be treacherous.

Here in the ward and away from the commotion of the emergency room, we needed to map out our new sleeping arrangements. We scouted the area; there was a set of benches, and we waited until nightfall to see what would happen. But soon, exhausted parents of children receiving care were sprawled out on them. It became clear that in the pediatric unit, they had priority over other accompanying relatives. One woman had just lost her infant child, so there was a lot of loud grieving. Another was on the verge of losing hers. Death seemed commonplace in this hospital.

Sally was among a small group of adult patients who were borrowing space from the pediatric unit, so we had to be tactful in our approach to securing a place to rest for the night. Sister Ra and Ndi decided to go back to the car, an SUV, and lay down. They had to roll down the windows because of the extreme heat and humidity, so mosquitoes became a distraction. That approach worked for a few hours, but then they found themselves back in the ward. They managed to find spots on the benches and slept sitting upright. A friendly nurse offered me a mattress from a broken bed in the lobby, and I took her up on it.

We brought blankets and bed sheets from home on the off chance that we might have to sleep on the floor. With the nurse's permission, I spread my blanket over the mattress and attempted to sleep. I asked the young boy assisting his aunt to come and join me. He had been sleeping in a chair in the room for the week that they'd been in the hospital. The poor boy seemed exhausted but had no choice but to stay. Life in the hospital was difficult for adults, and worse for children who had to serve as helpers.

I was eager to rest my head, but the little boy refused to share the mattress with me. His aunt urged him, letting him know that sleeping upright in the chair was not a good thing for a child. He finally obliged. He took his place on the rear of the mattress, facing the wall. He coiled up and went to sleep.

Wake-up time was about 5:30 a.m., when housekeeping staff started their daily activities or nurses came to check on patients. You also had to get up to fetch hot water from the kitchen or there'd be none left after 6 a.m. I had trouble waking up my little bedmate; he was relaxed and needed the comfort that a mattress on the floor offered. He finally stirred, and without a word walked off to fetch water. I smiled because he seemed happy in some small way.

I could see his vulnerability. He was a child, exhausted, tired of seeing sick people, and had no one to play with to relieve his stress. I learned the boy was a very good soccer player, a talent he had inherited from his dad, who could have made the national team if not for the lack of a sponsor. But here he was, alone, and no soccer ball to soothe his anxiety and loneliness. I looked at him and could his sense his feeling of abandonment by parents whom he thought had prioritized their own needs over his. He needed to just be a child, with a soccer ball by his feet. I determined I would get to know him.

Being a gifted dribbler of ideas myself, I knew we had something in common, and I was going to explore it, if only to keep myself engaged and a little removed from the calamity I felt brewing around me. In fact, I was so good at talking up this child that, before I knew it, he was fetching my water early in the morning too. By the end of our stay, he would become like my own child. He would go home with me after his hospital stay with his aunt and remains with my mother today. He is almost done with high school and plans to attend university. I look forward to ensuring he receives a good education. That's what he got for fetching water for me in my time of need.

CHAPTER TEN

Adult Medical Care in the Pediatric Ward

Basic Care Is Not Basic Here

WE FOUND OUT THAT, IN THIS ward, phlebotomists, those who draw blood, came twice a day, once in the morning and once in the afternoon, and picked up any orders the doctors had given. If blood was needed after those hours or in between their visits, family members had to take vials to the blood lab. Because we arrived late that first day in the ward, we missed the phlebotomist. Sally needed blood drawn, so we had to run around to find someone to do it. Since sister Ra and Ndi decided to stay with Sally to see the residents when they came to examine her, it fell to me to go to the blood bank to obtain vials or drop off whatever was needed. I took the lab order from the doctor and went across the street to a row of blue-colored offices that housed the blood lab's administrative office.

The process of paying for blood work was a demanding one. At the office, I handed my order to a staffer, only to be told I needed to pay for that particular panel elsewhere. I left confused but made my way to another building. When I arrived, I was told they only logged the request and that I needed to take it to yet another office. So I left that office feeling frustrated, not to mention tired and hungry. I followed the directions I'd been given to the blood bank, where they told me I needed to come back only after the blood had been drawn and that I should return to the place where I had first gone to pay. By this time, I was near tears and felt humiliated. Why did such a simple task require so many steps? I was becoming more aware how fragmented this system was, nothing like what I was used to. However, my tears were more for my Sally, as I became resigned to the fact this system might not be able to provide the care she desperately needed. I had not planned this out well; my heart was breaking inside me. Unsure and helpless, I continued to look for the right office.

Sally's roommate had a niece who worked in the administrative office of the blood lab. I would later discover that she had seen me talking to her aunt during one of her visits soon after our arrival in the ward, but I hadn't paid much attention to her. The young lady recognized me when I returned and offered to help. Instead of the runaround that I'd been enduring, she took my information, entered it into a ledger, and took the receipt next door to pay the bill. She came back and gave me a piece of paper to take to the blood bank. I was grateful and rushed off. A process that should have taken no more than ten minutes took about forty-five. I finally got the vial needed for the doctor to draw the blood and returned to the pediatric ward to wait for him.

Interestingly, nurses here are not allowed to draw blood; only doctors and phlebotomists were permitted to carry out this simple task. Hours later, I walked the blood back to the blood bank. But first, I had to repeat the earlier process.

I had to go to the administrative building, log the blood sample request, pay the fee, and then finally take the receipt and the blood to the blood bank. At least, now I knew where I was going. However, because of this exhaustive process, I didn't realize I had turned the vial upside down and it was leaking blood on the receipt in which the vial was wrapped. I had lost at least a quarter of the sample. A woman gave me a tissue to wipe the blood off my hands. I thought I would have to go through the entire process a third time, but luckily that wasn't necessary. They had enough blood to run whatever tests they needed. I asked if I could wait for the results but was told they would take about four hours and that I should come back. I left the blood bank and returned to Sally's room. I was exhausted and couldn't help wondering what happens to patients who did not have the money to have the test done, or relatives to help navigate the system.

New Set of Troubles

Doctors went on strike two days after we arrived in the pediatric ward. This meant no one was available to examine patients, order medications, set up IVs, or undertake other activities that only doctors can do. The consulting doctor had come around once to see Sally since the strike began but told us nothing about the surgery. It was obvious at this point that she wouldn't be having surgery that week because they needed about four days to prepare her. In fact, Sally would be in the ward for nearly two weeks before the doctors talked about getting her into surgery. By this time, the residents had returned and were triaging patients to be operated on quickly, in the event another strike was called. It never occurred to us that a strike meant care would come to a halt, even if you had just left the operating room. Consequences be damned!

The results of Sally's abdominal scan were also now in her chart. We had received feedback from our relatives in the United States and their physician colleagues and believed it was important for the doctors here to know we were informed consumers of health care and could better advocate for our little sister.

One stateside physician informed us that this was a simple blockage, requiring a routine surgical procedure. Another said the cause of the enlargement of the pyloric area was associated with an untreated bacterial infection. Another concurred with the first, saying it should not be a complicated surgery, and that the condition often occurred among children and was rarely seen in adults. However, one relative, the nurse practitioner, raised the alarm that we were dealing with cancer and that the condition was graver than we had been led to believe. We discounted his opinion, maybe because it seemed too heavy to deal with. We just didn't want to go there. It would mean Sally would have to undergo radiation or chemotherapy, neither of which I thought her body could handle. So we never returned his call. In any case, we still had to wait to hear from the physicians on the ground here in Nigeria.

The consulting physician finally came around to see Sally. He prescribed a few medications and asked us to purchase them. He was armed with CAT scan results but barely said anything about them. We resigned ourselves to the fact that the doctor was simply going to do his job and that my podiatrist friend would later explain the findings to me. We'd been watching Mamie Dorothy in the next bed receive frequent visits from her consulting doctor and his residents, about five in all. They went over her case about three times that week. In contrast, we received just one visit, three or four residents without the consulting physician, and they simply took Sally's history, checked the IV, discussed her case among themselves, and then rushed off to see other patients. They came because the consulting physician forced them to.

At times, we'd call the residents to come check on Sally because her injection site was swollen, her feet were swollen, or something else was amiss. More often than not, they didn't answer their phones or, if forced to respond by their head physician, would take forever to come, as if they were doing us a favor. They were on strike and therefore didn't have to do anything, while patients lay sick and in dire need of care. Perhaps we should have simply left the hospital at that point, since it was foreshadowing things to come.

Although we had now spent two weeks in the hospital, a surgery that was to be done on Friday would require preparation to start on Tuesday. Doctors also had their specific operating days, so that the rotation would cover all the scheduled surgeries. Our doctor's operating schedule was Mondays and Fridays, and we first had to wait for the doctors to return from their strike before Sally's surgery could be set. If they went on strike again, the entire system would shut down again, and all bets would be off.

The road to health in this system, it seemed, depended on having family members who could afford to pay for care; having family who were available to run around performing many menial tasks; have the good fortune of getting a doctor who knows what he is doing and cares enough to want to do it; having nurses with the freedom or latitude to undertake most tasks of patient care without the need to wait for a physician; and praying that the nation's doctors felt they were being properly compensated so they didn't need to strike while you were awaiting or recovering from surgery.

When I asked why doctors so easily went on strike, we were told that the governor had diverted funds meant for salaries into an interest-yielding account so he could collect the high interest for himself. We were told this was common practice. Many doctors leave the country as a result, and a few who shared that insight with us have also since left the country to practice medicine in Europe.

CHAPTER ELEVEN

Moving Along in the Care Process

The Reality of the Unknown

WE WERE TOLD WE HAD TO get a blood count for Sally to determine how much blood would be required for the surgery. Every surgical patient was required to get blood donated, at least a pint or two, or three pints if the patient was found to have low blood level prior to the procedure surgery. So patients had to enlist family members or pay strangers to donate blood for them. That process alone could take three days, as many of these families come from far-off villages and might have to be tested for compatibility. On occasion, the blood bank would allow individuals to buy blood, but these pints had to be replaced before the patient could leave the hospital, even if discharged. Ultimately, Sally had adequate blood count and would only need two pints of blood as a precautionary measure.

We had time for this and sent word back to the village so they could locate young men who could donate. Men, more than women, fulfilled this informal requirement. Our cousin Nedu, who was bringing us food in the hospital every couple of days, had a friend who lived in town and reached out to him for a blood donation. Ndi, who remained with us at the hospital, was also tested, as was a third cousin from our village. In the end, only two of the four people tested were compatible and could donate.

For those two weeks, we slept on cement floors, with mattresses from broken beds or blankets that we put on the floor. Once, I was able to go back to the village to get a good night's sleep, leaving sister Ra and Ndi to stay with Sally. I had become stressed out, as living conditions were not conducive for extended stays. Mama would send food from the village every other day, and we would try to eat food from local vendors on the other days. I was starting to get sick from eating poorly prepared foods from street vendors and local restaurants.

The week of the surgery, Sally was put on an IV again and was not allowed to eat anything, not that she would have been able to. We were not allowed to brush her teeth in the off chance that she would swallow the toothpaste foam. Three days before her surgery, they passed a tube into her stomach to remove excess stomach fluid. As before, getting the tube into her stomach through her nostril was a nightmare. Her body was starting to tire now. She hadn't been eating for three days, so nothing but greenish substances came out of her stomach.

Dr. Amyanna, a resident we had grown accustomed to seeing, reviewed Sally's chart. She examined the results of the abdominal scan, looked at me, and said, "It is not cancer, but there is a blockage, and we will fix it." I hadn't asked if it was cancer; she simply volunteered the information with an awkward stare that should have raised a red flag.

I sighed in relief. It didn't occur to me to panic that there was still a blockage that had to be dealt with. I took a walk, feeling elated and happy that the worst had not happened. She would be fine. I'm not sure why I felt that relieved, when I, too, had access to the CAT scan results. At the bottom of the findings, it said, "Malignant" with a question mark. I had previously read it in a cursory manner, perhaps afraid of what I would find. Then again, we'd sent the results to doctors in the United States, and they didn't raise any major concerns. Well, except for our one nurse practitioner-cousin, Vic. Hearing an actual, in-person doctor say no cancer made me happy. But it was a lie.

In any case, I returned to my senses and began wondering how they'd get rid of the blockage, whether cancerous or not. Her body was so fragile now. She had not eaten much in months. That meant her body chemistry was off, and she was malnourished. I wondered if she would survive the surgery. The truth that I had begun a simple journey through the maze of this very foreign health care system, without assurance that adequate care would be provided or that Sally even had the strength to survive surgery that was now imminent, had now become too real to me. Joy was beginning to give way to despair. I made calls to the United States to friends whom I knew were prayer warriors and asked for prayers. They were optimistic, and I hung on their every word.

My mother had come to visit Sally at the hospital a week after we got to the hospital. Sally looked "strong" then, in her words. But after the tube was inserted through her nostril, she started looking fragile again. *Can her frail body handle the intrusion into her body?* I thought, also wondered, what options, as we meandered through this unpredictable journey, had I failed to consider in my zeal to play hero and for a chance at a favorable outcome. Could I have simply joined everyone else saying, "Sally, eat your food," and not bothered to seek medical care, knowing that it offered no real solution to what was truly a major health problem? One of these doctors had removed a bullet from a man's head earlier, with only the scantiest of resources. Can one of them now remove a blockage from my Sally as well? I stared into oblivion, realizing there'd be no one to answer any of my questions.

The Imminence of Surgery and Its Complications

Two days prior to surgery, I got a call from one of the residents telling me that the consulting physician would like us to purchase a particular instrument to help with Sally's surgery. This was a stapler that was needed in lieu of sutures. We were told it would cost 138,000 Naira (about $693 USD), and that the need was urgent.

We needed to contact our siblings in the United States, first for them to approve the use of the stapler and then to send the money to pay for it. Sally's doctor decided it would hasten the recovery process and make the surgery far easier on her. He gave us the name of the vendor, who lived in Lagos but had suppliers in the city who worked closely with the FMC surgeons. The vendor told us there was already a stapler at the hospital, but it couldn't be used until they gave verbal approval after depositing the money in the vendor's bank account. We had forty-eight hours for our relatives to do the necessary research and to get the funds wired through Western Union.

The call came from my sister Di, the nurse, who said her physician colleagues thought it was a good idea and that we should move forward with the instrument. Now, the race to get the funds to us was on.

Nigeria was five hours ahead of the States at that time, in late April. That meant the Nigerian banks were already closed for the day when we received the call, leaving us just one day, the scheduled day of the surgery, to get the money wired. My siblings in the States mobilized that evening to send it, but we wouldn't receive it until the next morning. We called the vendor in Lagos to provide an update, but they wouldn't budge when we asked them to okay the use of the instrument on the promise of paying for it in the morning. It was confounding that something so critical for the performance of life-saving surgery was contingent on the whims of a private vendor. Why the hospital couldn't have purchased the stapler then simply billed patients for its use as part of the health care cost is beyond me.

At eight that morning, the vendor called to see if we'd deposited the money in their account, since the surgery was scheduled for ten. I told them my sister was at the bank, and there was a line as others were trying to cash Western Union money transfers. Nine came and went with no word, and I got another call from the vendor, who'd given me their account number earlier. I was getting frantic at this point. At 9:30 a.m., my sister received the money but was waiting in another line to deposit it, and it would likely be another hour.

I gave the vendor a play-by-play of what was going on. He said to simply call him with the deposit number when the transaction was completed, and he'd call the physician. At 9:45 a.m., Dr. Agamop, who'd be performing the surgery, walked past us into the operating room. I was on the phone with my sister, so I didn't notice him until he was closing the door and missed the chance to tell him to go ahead with the stapler because payment for the device was in the works.

My sister finally called at 10:30 a.m. to let me know that the transaction was complete and that she had called the vendor herself. I began calling to confirm they had authorized the use of the instrument, but for the next thirty minutes I couldn't get through. Suddenly, they weren't answering their phone. More frantic, I assumed the procedure had gone ahead without the stapler. Finally, at 11:00 a.m., the vendor called and said they'd been in a meeting earlier and couldn't get to the phone but would alert the doctor. I panicked because I wasn't sure the surgery had not yet started and was afraid the doctor may not have gotten the okay to use the instrument. He wouldn't be answering the phone if the surgery had begun. But I remained hopeful that all the running around hadn't been in vain.

Sister Ra was back now, and we were becoming convinced it had all been a scam. Nonetheless, we looked at each other and continued hoping for the best. I wouldn't know the outcome until much later.

The Quest for the Divine Presence

The day of the surgery, our mother arrived early to be with Sally. Unfortunately, she'd missed her by a few minutes when Sally was wheeled into the theater. She had been transported by ambulance at nine that morning, and I accompanied her, even helping put her on the stretcher. It was a short drive to the operating room. Ndi followed on foot, as sister Ra had left earlier for the bank.

It is noteworthy that this facility looked modern, and the floor of the OR was immaculately clean. This area was also well air-conditioned, which wasn't the case with other parts of the hospital, where the heat was often oppressive. I also have to acknowledge that the hospital always had electricity during our stay. Even if the power went out, a generator would immediately kick in.

When we arrived, I was not allowed to go past a certain point, and the receptionist handed me paperwork to fill out, after which I was told to sit outside in the visitors waiting area. Ndi had arrived, and we joined several other relatives waiting on their loved ones and rooting for them to make it out of the OR alive.

Nigeria is a religious country, and some family members huddled together in prayer groups, singing and praising God. This was especially common in a city where nothing was taken for granted, and everything depended on His divine intervention. In this system of care, where man's efforts were so limited, surrendering to God creates a sense that what man cannot do, the Creator has the capacity to do. So I huddled with strangers in total surrender and began to pray, still clutching the papers I was required to fill out.

CHAPTER TWELVE

The Next Phase: Post-surgery

Biopsy in a Bucket

ABOUT THREE HOURS LATER, SALLY WAS out of the operating room. I thought the time was especially short, given the nature of what they thought was wrong. After all, the doctor had the results of the scan.

Dr. Amyanna, who had told me earlier not to worry about cancer, called me into the entrance of the theater. She asked me to sign a few more papers acknowledging that Sally had completed surgery, and then handed me two plastic buckets, one large and one medium, containing tissue from the affected area. She was not pleasant and didn't look me in the eye. We were suddenly strangers. She was mechanical as she asked me to take the tissue to the lab for testing. It seemed as though she was withholding something. This was supposed to have been a routine operation; I did not understand why I was holding two relatively large buckets of tissue in my hands.

Since it apparently fell to the patient's family to transport their own loved one's tissue, it was necessary for other relatives to stay close by. I was tempted to open one of buckets but feared contaminating its contents. So I obeyed and took them as directed to the lab, which was a few blocks away, down a hill from the surgical theater. I was just happy Sally was out, and I no longer had to worry that she would die in surgery.

Sister Ra offered to come with me, and I asked the guard for directions, as I'd been in a confused state the first time someone gave them to me. When we arrived, a receptionist asked us to fill out forms and then go to another building several blocks away to pay the biopsy fee before they could send the contents to the lab. Always the need to go to different locations to pay bills, receive receipts, and what have you! Perhaps it was their way of keeping their staff honest.

I left the two containers sitting on the table, unrefrigerated, for what seemed like an eternity. In fact, it was over an hour before sister Ra returned from paying the biopsy fee so they could record the containers and take them in for testing. There was much ado around the table as other family members tried to register their own containers for testing. We were later told by a resident that the biopsy was needed to ascertain the stage of the disease with which Sally had been diagnosed. Stage of the disease? The surgeon had not told us it was cancer; the only resident who truly took a liking to Sally said it was not cancer; and no other staff doctor had given us a true indication of what was happening or what to expect. I considered myself a knowledgeable and informed consumer of health care, yet I was ignored at every turn and walked through that health care system just as any illiterate person would have. In this system of care, doctors are tin gods, and they alone decide what you should know or not. It was at that moment that the enormity of Sally's condition hit home.

After being told the biopsy would take a week, sister Ra and I returned to the theater. They were getting ready to transport Sally back to the ward, where she was expected to fully recover. Nonetheless, I was concerned. I thought they would send her to recover in the theater area or place her in a special room nearby, and only transport her when she was out of the woods. Yet here she was, still unconscious, being sent back to the ward. I was told this was normal. It was a frightening prospect, and you will soon see why.

A Mother's Love in Time of Dire Need

Sally was out of the operating room, sedated and unconscious. The ambulance to take her back to the ward arrived and drove her the few blocks back, along with a resident in attendance. When Sally got to the ward, the resident and the driver wheeled her into her room. I had no part in the process this time. Suddenly, there were four nurses and three residents surrounding her bed, working feverishly to resuscitate her. Sally was ice cold. It occurred to me that the scene looked like something out of the old CBS series *MASH*. The comedy, which ran from

1972–1983, was set in the Korean War and involved a team of American doctors and support staff who were stationed at a remote army hospital there. This was 2015, and the nature of postsurgical care I was observing at that moment in a Nigerian hospital reminded me of a 1950s' mobile army surgical hospital in time of war. I panicked, and in that moment, I knew Sally was in trouble.

They pumped in quick succession two bags of IV fluids through her veins, pressing on the bags so that their contents would drain very fast into her body. It was as though she was drinking water through her vein. They then began calling out her name, trying to wake her up. She didn't respond, though seven medical staff hovered around her bed.

Our mother, who had been told to wait outside, sprang up on her heels, realizing that her daughter was not responding. Sally was in crisis, and she needed her mother. Nothing in that moment gave us hope that Sally would recover from the surgery. One of the doctors asked Mama to leave, but she refused. As they asked her again, she let out a loud scream, "Salome!" and immediately Sally responded in a thin voice, "Maman?" What a mother's love can do! My mother answered her back, and the doctors again began furiously trying to keep her awake. My mother then rejoined us back outside, where we were peeking through the closed curtain to see what was going on.

I thank God for mothers. We sometimes forget their value and focus our attention on what we think they are doing wrong. God answered her cry for immediate help. Sally would live to see another day, but we were now bracing for postsurgical complications.

Adult Care in the Pediatric Ward

We all sat near the window, and the curtain was pulled to shade Sally from prying eyes outside. All was quiet now. We knew she had made it through the worst. We now waited to see if the surgery was a success. The truth about what had actually happened in the operating room had not been revealed to us, so we naively thought that Sally would now have a chance at a normal life. All she needed to do now was recover. I breathed a sigh of relief, having had this discussion between my brain and my heart, settling on the conclusion that we had done the right thing. Perhaps, I thought, my visit home was meant to take care of Sally. A sense of accomplishment suddenly overwhelmed my heart. I bowed my head and said a little prayer of thanks.

When she finally became responsive, the three male residents handed her case over to the nurses and began filing out of the room. One stayed behind to explain to me what had happened. Unlike other cases, where they would all have just left without any explanation, they knew I was different and that I demanded information. This resident told me plainly, without hesitation, that my sister had a year and a half to live and that the problem had not been eliminated, since her body could not handle extensive surgery. They had simply bypassed the blocked area, creating another opening to allow her to eat. But that opening had required them to take out a large chunk of another body part—which part he did not say—and that's what I'd carried to the lab in two buckets. The problem was still there, and she just needed to go home and try to eat soft foods until her death.

This was the first time we were formally told it was cancer, and that there was no hope of recovery. I was perplexed. Let this sink in for a moment: we wouldn't have learned any of this if not for one young doctor that found it in his heart to be forthcoming with us. The surgeon clearly had not planned to release any details of the surgery or Sally's prognosis.

I took a deep breath and wondered if we had done the right thing to have had the surgery. I thought, *Now she has to deal with recovery and a surgical scar that might not heal well because of her malnourished condition. Health care in this country does not adequately address pain management, so there would be nothing to help her deal with the pain after she left the hospital.* I believed she was in far worse condition now than before the surgery. My heart sank. I felt like I had betrayed her. My hero worship expectation was now all gone. I hadn't swooped in to save the day, it now seemed. Sally trusted me. She would always look at me, call me by my pet name, and then smile. I would say, "Sally, do you love me?" What a question to ask! Sally would casually give me a smile that would melt any soul, and then nod her head. Her eyes always revealed love for all her siblings.

I remember one particular instance—of course, there were many others—when I had fallen asleep and apparently was having some kind of difficulty as I slept. While other siblings didn't notice anything amiss, it was our "eagle eye" Sally who saw that I was in trouble. It was her insistent and loud shouting of "Holy Ghost take control of my sister, she's in trouble, she can't breathe," over and over, and either her shouting or the Holy Ghost finally woke me up. Now, here, I felt ashamed that

I had betrayed that trust. I hadn't called out to the Holy Ghost to take control of her life. I sank into the bed next to Sally.

A Promise to One of God's Special Ones

When we were waiting for a bed in the emergency room, I had promised Sally that when she felt better and got healed, she would go to church and give praise to God. She loved dancing to praise music, so I promised her we would get the band at church to play her favorite song as she danced. I was losing hope now, and fear had overtaken me. I thought, *Would Sally ever dance in church again?*

The next day, I shared with Dr. Amyanna, the one who treated me like a stranger after the surgery, that her colleague had told us Sally had cancer and had only about eighteen months to live. She was furious and said there was no reason that should have been shared with us. She answered that only God Almighty can put a timeline on any individual's life. It is noteworthy that doctors here are not accustomed to telling patients either their diagnoses or prognoses, so this put her in an uncomfortable position. Indeed, it was the hospital's policy not to divulge such information, at least not in any detail. I was an exception because they knew I was from America, and they were dealing with someone who operated on the same need-to-know level that they were.

In her zeal to make me feel better, the doctor noted that someone she knew had been diagnosed with terminal cancer and ended up outliving the doctor who diagnosed him and that

that individual was still alive today. Then she paused and asked, "Why didn't you purchase the stapler?"

I panicked upon realizing at that moment that all the effort to get the stapler to them had failed. I told her we indeed had bought the instrument and explained everything we went through to get it put to use by the surgeon. She nodded and said maybe it was used after all; she'd had to leave Sally's operating room to attend to another patient and hadn't been there for the conclusion. I suspected she was just backpedaling for my benefit. My heart sank. I wondered what would happen to Sally since the instrument that might have made her life easier had not been used.

Dr. Agamop rarely came to see his patient, but when he finally visited, I asked him what happened with the stapler. He acknowledged that he hadn't used it but offered no explanation. He wasn't much of a talker. We knew we'd be calling the vendor in Lagos and demanding our money back. There was a serious confrontation, but we weren't taking no for an answer. The process of getting our money took two weeks, but they finally wired it to sister Ra's account. That money was later used to pay for the rest of Sally's stay in the hospital.

CHAPTER THIRTEEN

Treacherous Post-surgery Journey: Doctors' Second Strike

Where Do We Turn?

SALLY'S RECOVERY FROM SURGERY WAS VERY slow. We had to pay for every drug that was prescribed and had to do so before they could be given to her. She was given two pints of blood, one of which was still attached to her hand when she was wheeled back to her room. Hours later, she began reacting to the blood transfusion. She had rashes and black spots on different parts of her body. She was being monitored for further reactions. What was frightening was that during the twenty-four hours that she was being given blood, she could not get any pain medication, so as not to mask any adverse reactions to the transfusion.

Suddenly, Sally began to scream. The pain medication she'd received during surgery was now wearing off. She began to move violently as though she was going to tear the IV needle out of her arm. We screamed for the nurses, and Dr. Amyanna was also in the area. She came in and told the nurses to stop the transfusion and give her pain meds. Had she not received them, she would have fallen on the floor in pain and torn the stitches from the surgery. As it was, she'd begun secreting blood from the surgical area into a bag that was attached by a tube. As I write this story, I am still saddened by the memory of her pain.

Sally was on antibiotic, which we were told would be given three times a day intravenously. Not surprisingly, the nurses could not deal with any medication and procedure that had to be administered by IV. Those procedures were left to doctors; they could only dress wounds, give tablet medications, make the beds, and adjust IV bags. I asked later why nurses weren't involved with more sophisticated medical procedures, and one doctor said there'd been many fatalities from bad intravenous placements and other more delicate procedures, so the system determined only doctors should undertake these tasks. In effect, nurses might be sitting around in the office while a patient went into cardiac arrest, and they'd have to wait for a doctor before the patient could be resuscitated. To me, this was a gross undermining of nurses' skills and acumen, and something that must be reevaluated. The perception that they could not effectively be trained to give IV or take on more delicate roles underestimates the intelligence of these wonderful creations of God.

Although she was supposed to be on the antibiotic, on some days Sally had no medication because the resident failed to arrive, as another strike had begun two days after her surgery. The reason for this strike? Nurses were now allowed to serve as consultants after several years of service. This was the second doctor strike during our stay at the hospital; the only reason we were still here was because of the first one, which delayed Sally's surgery for nearly two weeks. This time, the doctors would be out for even longer, leaving no one to treat patients. Nurses had been relegated to doing menial tasks, and more technical ones like giving drugs via IV were left undone. The nurses tried their best to fill in for the doctors but could only comfort patients and provide those in pain oral pain medications.

On one occasion, Sally was experiencing excruciating pain, and the hand containing the IV was badly swollen. I tried calling the consulting physician for hours to let him know what was happening, since the residents were on strike. He promised to come but never did. Then, about nine hours later, a resident who worked in the emergency room visited, apparently having been called by the consulting physician. ER physicians, it seemed, did not go on strike.

Of the three physicians who came to see Sally during the long strike, two worked in the emergency room and the other was Dr. Amyanna, who had taken a liking to us. Indeed, had it not been for this compassionate doctor, Sally would have gone without the IV fluids that contained nutrients she needed. I had to go to town to buy a box of IV bags, lest Sally starve to death.

Medical Care When Doctors Are on Strike

Sally had a rough week after her surgery. A bag had been attached to a tube that was inserted in the surgical opening. This was supposed to collect extra fluid from her body, but Sally was draining large amounts of bloody fluid, and with doctors on strike there was nothing anyone could do. The nurses asked us to phone the doctors directly to come and assess the situation, since they rarely responded to nurses' calls. Nonetheless, these doctors tended not to answer their phones or would tell us they were on their way and never show up. Also disheartening was that, after the surgery, it took several days for Dr. Agamop to come see Sally. A few conscientious residents came around to help, even though their colleagues were on strike.

Since I had developed a personal relationship with the consulting physician, I continued pestering him to come examine Sally. By this time, not only were her legs, but also her hands were swollen, and she was beginning to secrete even more fluid into the drainage bag. At times, the bed would be soaked with blood, and she would have to be moved gingerly so the nurses could change the sheets. Mind you, for days after the surgery, Sally still had the tube attached to her nostril to drain fluid from her stomach. The nurse would measure the fluid collected to determine if it was increasing or decreasing, and thereby whether to remove that tube altogether. Day and night, they would drain the bag attached to the tube running from her nostril. This meant Sally had to lie on her left side most of the time, or on occasion on her back so her body would not disrupt the flow of fluid. She also could not walk around, which was delaying her recovery.

Dr. Amyanna, although still on strike, came to visit out of concern. She observed that Sally's condition was deteriorating and became frantic when she saw she was losing blood at the site of the surgical scar. She requested a new blood count; it seemed obvious to her that Sally would need additional blood transfusion. She would put in the request herself, but one of us would have to go and pay for it at the administrative billing office, return with the paid receipt, and then go to the blood bank to pick up vials. When this was accomplished, she would draw the blood, take it to the lab, and run the test herself. Other approaches would take at least twenty-four hours, and Sally didn't seem to have that much time if she needed blood. Indeed, lab technicians normally visited the wards only in the morning and early afternoon. The afternoon tech had already come and gone and wouldn't return until the next day. So the only other way to get Sally's blood tested was for the doctor to do it herself. It was a kind offer.

Sister Ra once again took on this errand. She came back with the paid receipt, and true to her word, Dr. Amyanna took the blood to the lab. After several hours, she returned and told us that Sally's blood count was normal, and that she would not need an additional transfusion. The fluid coming out of the surgical scar on her right side was still mixed with blood and seemed to be nonstop. It's worth noting that even after Sally left the hospital, the local doctor had to come drain fluid from that side of her body because it had nowhere to go. Sally's surgical wound would never heal.

The doctors remained on strike and Sally was missing several doses of her medications. But on occasion, one very good doctor would stop by to do what she could, such as changing the site of her IV since her hand was often swollen in that area. Sally was in the hospital for two weeks post-surgery, and her biopsy results had not come back. We were told we'd have them in a week, but the strike brought everything to a standstill. Further, it is uncertain what purpose the results would have served since she was not getting any special treatment anyway. Moreover, her body did not seem particularly suited for chemotherapy. One resident had recommended it but noted she wouldn't tolerate it well. The surgery did not go well, and adding chemotherapy on top of it did not look like a logical next step.

A week after the tube in her nostril was removed I decided to begin taking Sally for short walks. I would hold her IV stand, and we'd amble around the ward. We did that for two days. The walks were very slow, but Sally's ability to move about well gave us some hope. By the third day, I noticed little children were frightened to see an adult attached to machines walking around their ward, so we stopped and just allowed Sally to move back and forth in her tiny room.

I now had to return to the United States. I was worried that things would go from bad to worse since many of the doctors who came to help had done so because of me, as they were still technically on strike. I had already extended my stay twice. Sally spent another week in the hospital after my departure, and at the time she was discharged had been there for five weeks.

CHAPTER FOURTEEN

Indigent Patients: The Loss of Any Semblance of Quality Care

No Payment, No Treatment

EVERY WEEK, SOMEONE FROM ADMINISTRATION WOULD come around asking patients to pay for their beds and other medical expenses. If a patient did not or could not pay for the week's stay, their medical chart would be picked up by the billing clerk and taken to the administrative office. Exasperatingly, their chart would not be returned until they or family visited the administrative office, which was located at the front end of the ward, to pay the bill. You read that right: care would be suspended for patients who were unable to pay for their stay, leaving them to languish in the hospital, sometimes deprived of critical care for a full week. These included surgical patients, needing wound care, antibiotics, IVs, and other medical assistance.

The chart of the patient who shared the room with Sally was taken from her because she had not paid for her care for the week. Mamie Dorothy had a mastectomy and could not afford to pay the second bill after paying the initial bill the week before. Her debt was 48,000 Naira (about $241 USD). They had not removed her bandage, and her wound was bleeding. She was also in constant pain, but no one would attend to her because she owed the hospital money. This patient was now facing two issues: the doctors were on strike and could not come around to assess her situation, and the nurses could not provide even the most basic care because she had not paid for her second week.

Mamie Dorothy's wound had been treated the day before the doctors went on strike, so they would not be coming around to check on her again anytime soon. It was up to the nurses, should they choose, to dress her wound and provide any tablet medications from the hospital pharmacy, which they'd leave in a small sachet in a bag tied to the bedrail at the foot of her bed. One nurse dressed her wound the day before administration came to check on payment status, but did not do a very good job, and the bandage was now falling apart. She tried unsuccessfully to get any of the other nurses to redo the bandage, eventually resorting to covering the area with her traditional wrap until a nurse with some compassion came and took care of it for her. Finally, the next day, a very kind nurse who had just started her rotation on the ward only that day and who, at that time, was going off duty, heard her plea for assistance and decided to attend to her needs. She was able to borrow gauze and other supplies from another patient and properly wrapped the wound to prevent any leakage.

Mamie Dorothy also could not receive any of her medications other than the tablets left in the sachets, because no one had instructions on how to administer them. The names of the medications did not often appear on the sachets because, I was told, patients might try to buy them without a doctor's order if they became sick, especially if they thought they had the same ailment that brought them into the hospital.

Medications bought by patients' families were placed in little containers also at the foot of the bed. Nurses and doctors would look at the chart, and then search the container for the particular medication needed at that time. Even in instances where a patient's chart had been removed because of failure to pay, some nurses would comb through the container to see what they could give the patient to help. Sometimes, if the patient was literate, they could search the container themselves and find the medication they needed.

Mamie Dorothy gave me medications from the bag at the foot of her bed to read and instruct her on how they should be taken. Some sachets had obvious instructions; others did not. I read them to her but recommended she wait for the nurse who re-dressed her wound to come and help her. I found the nurse outside, and being a God-fearing woman, she accompanied me back in the room. She took a few medications from the pile and gave them to her patient. Mamie Dorothy would wait three more days before she could get additional help; however, she had made a note of what the nurse had given her and self-medicated twice a day until help came and her bill was paid.

Also troubling, and as noted earlier, was that patients were not allowed to go home after their discharge until they had paid their bill in full, including cost of medications, bed, food, and supplies. It was not uncommon for a patient to remain in the hospital for another week or two after medical discharge. This meant that beds weren't available to other patients who might desperately need them. At least in this particular federal hospital, patients could remain in their beds and not be shunted off to floor like in the village hospital.

Another reason a patient could not be released, even though they were fit to go home, was failure to donate replacement blood to the blood bank if they had received blood during surgery or at any time during their stay. Only rarely were patients allowed to compensate the blood bank with cash.

Hospital beds were being tied up all over the wards because of these policies, and those who needed a bed were either asked to go home and come back in a few days or, if they came in through the emergency room, were kept there until beds became available. It is worth noting that some patients died without getting a bed, others became discouraged and left the hospital for traditional practitioners, and still others went further into debt as their release was delayed while scrambling to find someone to pay their hospital bill. This is why adult patients end up sharing pediatric wards with sick children.

Mamie Dorothy ran up against all these problems: she had failed to pay her medical bill for the week, she did not have money to settle her medical bill in full, and she needed to replace a pint of blood that had been given to her during her recovery from surgery. Eventually, a Good Samaritan provided funds to pay the bill, but she remained in the hospital for a total of five days after discharge, three of which were spent trying to find someone to donate a pint of blood.

CHAPTER FIFTEEN

Care Details Post-surgery

Wound Care: A Complicated Simple Task

THE NURSES DID THEIR BEST TO dress Sally's wound, asking us to buy the supplies they needed. Even that seemingly simple act was often a tedious one. First, the doctor would write the prescription for the supplies. You'd then take the script to the supply store within the hospital to get clearance. Next, you'd have to take it to the billing center, where you would be told the cost and pay the bill, after which you'd take the receipt back to the nursing station. Only then would the charge nurse send another nurse to obtain the needed items. If it happened to be their break time, you'd have to wait until they returned from break before the supplies could be obtained.

It's worth noting that, even after collecting the supplies, there might still be a wait before a nurse would take care of the patient's wound. Also irritating was the fact that the entire process had to be repeated as many times as was required to take care of the patient; ordering a week's worth of supplies ahead of time just didn't happen.

This Byzantine process occurred about ten times during the week I spent with Sally in the hospital before returning to the United States. When the needed supplies were not available in the hospital store, someone would have to go to town to buy them. It was exhausting.

Recovery and Feeding Post-surgery

It took a week after surgery before Sally was allowed to start eating solid foods. It was also during this time that I began lifting her from her bed and taking her for walks in the corridor so she could ambulate. We would walk ever so slowly, but it helped in her recovery. She also started using the bathroom on her own, leaving behind the bed pan, which she hated and often refused to use. Going to the bathroom on her own made Sally feel better about herself, and the smile returned to her face. I brushed her teeth using small amounts of toothpaste, and then used Listerine to give her mint-fresh breath. She was fastidious about her daily hygiene. Indeed, under normal circumstances, she would not speak to anyone in the morning until she had brushed her teeth, so to be in a position where she couldn't handle that small routine really angered her.

In the days prior to her surgery, when the draining bag was attached to her nostril, she demanded that we brush her teeth. However, we were told she was not to swallow anything, nor even spit out the toothpaste. So I learned to put Listerine on a tissue and rub it on her teeth. I brought a traveler's size with me from the United States, and it came in handy. Getting her teeth cleaned this way pleased her, but now she was able to gargle and rinse her mouth by herself, aiding in her sense of recovery and making us all smile.

I left for the United States the day they introduced solid foods to Sally. They started slowly with liquids and then light meals. I was always concerned with what would happen when they stopped the IV fluids and how she would fare with solid foods, even if soft. It was unclear how she would react, particularly since her wound was still draining bloody fluid. This meant other parts of her body, particularly the new surgical pathway created inside of her (which we never learned the details of), may also have been draining bloody fluid. I was skeptical how effective this new opening could be, as this health care system had not revealed any hint of sophistication to me. I recalled the two pails of tissue I carried to lab for biopsy after her surgery. My head felt like it would explode.

While in transit home from Germany, I got a call saying Sally had vomited everything she had eaten that first day. We were back to praying for things to change; after everything, Sally still could not hold food down in her stomach. During the week she spent in the hospital without me, she only kept down food less than two days, and that was mostly just liquids. We feared her problem had not been corrected, and on top of that,

Sally now had to deal with constant pain from an incision in her stomach. What's more, even the doctors were unsure of the cause of the bloody leakage or how to deal with it. My guess was that she was now malnourished, making it a struggle for her body to heal. The poorly performed surgery didn't help matters.

Discharge Home and Follow-Up Care

Sally went home because there was nothing more the doctors could do for her. In fact, they were still on strike two weeks after her surgery, and there were none to regularly visit her in the ward to monitor her condition. She'd still have to go back as an outpatient to have her wound dressed. This task fell on our sister Ra the following week, and since the doctors remained on strike, they saw the consulting doctor, who was now running the clinic by himself.

It was now six weeks since the surgery, and the results of the biopsy still hadn't been shared with us. I called the consulting physician from the United States to see what he could do. He insisted he was trying to get through to the lab, but with the strike, everything had ground to a halt. I would continue to call him to inquire, but nothing happened. It was unclear what difference having the results would make, but it would be good to know what the findings were.

Sally went to the clinic at the hospital to see the consulting physician one more time, but by the third week after being released, she started to deteriorate. She was throwing up everything, and the sutured area was continuously filled with fluid.

She had no strength to make the long journey to the city to see the doctor at his clinic, for either her wound care or general consultation. It occurred to us that the doctor himself did not know what to do at this juncture. Sister Ra bought a mobile walker for Sally to use for moving around. She also started experiencing severe pain, and loss of leg strength.

I made arrangements for Sally to return to the local hospital for the doctor there to follow up with her care. He had the consulting physician's phone number, so they could discuss her case and determine the right course of action. This doctor, a very close family friend, was saddened to see how fast Sally was fading. He was surprised to hear we had still not obtained the biopsy results but felt that the surgery had not been done right. In fact, he said, perhaps there had been no need for the surgery since her body did not seem healthy enough for an invasive procedure. He was regretful that he even initiated the process that landed us at the feet of doctors who did not seem to either care or know much. Nonetheless, he agreed to monitor Sally while at home.

CHAPTER SIXTEEN

Returned to Home Care: A Farewell

The End of a Sad Journey

S ALLY STARTED TO HAVE SLEEPLESS NIGHTS. Her pain got worse. The hospital did not give her pain medication to take home. The local doctor noticed she had lost much of her body weight because she was still not eating and began sending nurses to give Sally IV fluids at home. We preferred home care; even though the local hospital was a smaller facility, and the nurses here were far more involved in taking care of their patients, someone would still have to stay overnight, as her condition was delicate. Moreover, the hospital environment was unhealthy for non-patients, and sleeping on the floor was intolerable. So we opted to have the nurses come provide home care for Sally and were willing to shoulder the extra cost involved.

Before long, the nurses were giving her intravenous pain medications with the approval of the doctor, who did not feel intimidated and did not mind the nurses assuming more active roles in patient care. But now, these were not helping. The meds would wear off in less than an hour, and she would begin to scream like an animal in pain. She would howl so loudly people who lived far away could hear her. She was keeping the entire village awake. There was no method of pain management; the consulting physician in the city had briefed the local doctor on what to do, but nothing proved adequate.

Sally had no stamina and would fall if she attempted to stand or use the bathroom. So sister Ra bought a support stand. After two weeks of severe pain, there was no more resemblance of the Salome we knew. Her appearance and countenance had changed, and the lack of nutrients in her body meant she had lost most of her body weight. She was starting to look like a wild animal, and we could not help her. In an effort to balance life with Sally now, those around her began taking short naps during the day to make up for sleepless nights.

Sally's biopsy results finally came two months after her surgery. At this point, there was no need to see them. They indicated Stage II cancer, which would mean that Sally had at least one and a half years to live or would not die at all, but she had all the symptoms of Stage IV cancer, and everyone knew she was dying. She still could not hold any food down because whatever artificial opening the doctor had created in the operating room was now nothing but a source of additional pain. Her body was eating itself. She had lost her muscle strength. She also developed liver and kidney problems. Her body was shutting down.

Compassionate Care

Had Sally been in the United States, the surgery would have gone differently. And, on the off chance that it did not, she would have received hospice care or palliative care. Here, our friendly local doctor was now sending nurses to the house more frequently to help stabilize her and make the pain bearable. But the meds only lasted about fifteen minutes each time, and then the howling would begin again. They would also dress her wound, but the wounds inside of her could not be dressed. Sally was experiencing continuous excruciating pain, and nothing helped.

Nighttime became a terror zone. Sally suffered greatly. Her wounds were oozing, and she was physically rotting away. She was now emitting a foul odor. She continued to howl and scream like an animal sent to slaughter; nothing could stop her pain, not even morphine. It was a nightmare for the whole family. I'm told our mother was now releasing long sighing sounds, reflective of one who was out of options. When I called Mama from the United States, I was racked with guilt. A mother was watching her child die and had no ability to help ease her suffering.

One of the best things that medical care in the United States has to offer is pain management. The value of this capability, even or especially for those who are dying, cannot be truly measured until you have looked into the face and eyes of someone whose pain level is beyond the number ten on the pain scale. Pain of unmatched intensity has the potential of stripping one of their humanity.

The screaming and shrieking were particularly hard on our father, who was sick himself and felt as helpless as we all did. He called out to God for help, while shouting at Sally to stop screaming. The entire household came to a halt, with no solution in sight. More troubling, you could see that Sally was no longer there. Something else had taken over.

Seven weeks after she returned home from the hospital, I asked my sister to take Sally to the village hospital, believing they could better manage her pain there. As soon as she arrived, they put her on IV pain meds. Her screaming stopped, and she looked better after just a few hours. We thought there might still be hope—that a miracle could happen.

Several hours later, Sally died. We were deeply saddened by her sudden death, but she was no longer in pain. She did not live to see the one and a half years that the doctors had predicted, or dance again in gratitude to the Lord in church, or look once more at her little girl, whom she so desperately wanted to see before dying. My father, whose heart must have broken to lose this special child, would not see Sally's corpse. He, too, would die, several months later.

Sally died just shy of two months after her surgery. The doctor in the village was disappointed with the health care system. When he first encountered Sally and her stomach problems, nothing in her blood work had indicated Stage IV cancer or that she would die within weeks of surgery that was supposed to save her. I don't know what they could have done differently given their knowledge, skills, and resources, but I am aware that the surgery was an abject failure. It was not properly done, and it not only did not correct the problem, but also added to her misery. The doctor who performed it lacked compassion and decency.

The system had failed Sally: doctors were frequently on strike for no legitimate reason, medications were not given to patients at the appointed time because of the strike, surgical wounds were inadequately cared for because no one was paying attention and let them become infected, and doctors weren't paying enough attention to ensure their surgeries were successful. We had no idea what opening Dr. Agamop made inside of Sally to help her, but post-surgery, she was still unable to eat, and that wound added a new dimension to her already precarious situation. It seemed that Sally was simply cut open, had parts taken out, was sutured back together, and then was left to rot away. A few long trips back to the clinic at the hospital where she had her surgery, to tend to her wounds, yielded only stress.

It is relevant to note that many other patients died in that hospital because of the doctors' strike and poor care. It began in the emergency room with no defibrillators to resuscitate dying patients and ended with doctors who were not present, further compromising the poor care offered to patients. The "belief in himself only" surrounding Sally's surgeon was itself a problem. He was the "be all and end all," and there was no one to put a check on his seeming lack of empathy or nonexistent concern for the well-being of his patients. Yet, patients were expected to consider themselves privileged to receive care from him because he was supposedly the best. I shudder to think what the "not the best" ones looked like.

CHAPTER SEVENTEEN

A Sister's Love That Wasn't Enough

Reflections

I WAS HAUNTED FOR A WHILE ABOUT Sally's death. I asked myself many times why I hadn't thought of going to the American embassy in Abuja, applying for a visa for Sally, and returning to the United States with her. The process of obtaining a visa is a tedious one under the best circumstances; the wait for an interview can be two months. Sally had no passport, not even a birth certificate, so it would have been daunting. But perhaps she would have qualified for an expedited visa given her dire circumstances. It's not uncommon for the American embassy to issue such a visa, but my failure to pursue this option remains a heartbreaking thought for me to this day. Why this course of action didn't cross my mind, I'll never know. Yes, she might have died while waiting for a visa interview, and even if she was ultimately rejected, that would have been out of my control. But I could have tried. Whatever might have transpired, Sally's last months might have been less traumatic had surgery not been performed. In a small way, I too failed her.

Sally will be missed. When she was younger, when you asked her name, she'd say, "Chokomy." So, Chokomy, as Adanne would lovingly call you when you'd lean on her shoulder, we are bidding you farewell. May you rest in perfect peace, in the bosom of God Almighty. Through your stay at the general hospital we got to meet Gemezu, the young man who was tending to your roommate, Mama Dorothy. I remember meeting his father when he came to pick up your roommate after her release from the hospital. He told me he had four other sons living in a two-room house in a remote village, and that he wanted a better life for his eldest. He asked me to take Gemezu home with me. Although by this time the twelve-year-old had gone from unpleasant stranger to dear friend, I told him I live in America and had no way of taking his son with me. He asked if I would ask my mother to take him, so he would be raised by our family.

Gemezu would be brought to Mama after I left for America and go on to become a very important part of our family. He seems to be on his way to having a great future. He is almost done with his secondary school education, and I have plans to send him to the university. He tells me he wants to become a doctor. It is my prayer that his life will make history in Nigeria, as I believe the Lord God Almighty will anoint his hands for healing, and his heart for compassionate care. I pray that there will be more like him in Nigeria's future.

When I saw him a few months later, during my return trip home for your funeral, he ran to me, gave me a big hug, and screamed, "Mommy, you are back!" He had a special place in his heart for me, one that remains until this day. Your death would dampen our reunion, but he was glad to see me, nonetheless. Gemezu cried for you, touched by your brief hospital encounter and the deep friendship that quickly developed after your discharge from the hospital. He was among those who cared for the delicate human being you'd become because of your illness and remains a very good companion for Mama. See how something good has already blossomed from your journey through the Nigerian health care system, Sally? We are grateful. I believe there is still more to come. In fact, though your life was short, we are hopeful that you did not die in vain, that your story will cause the Nigerian Government and other stakeholders to take a hard look at its health care system.

When we look at how poorly doctors there are treated, after they invest years in time and money in their studies, it is time to take politics out of the profession and move it to a place of reason, conscience, and compassion. The doctor who treated Sally and performed her endoscopy had to travel abroad for medical conferences, to learn whatever new techniques he sought to elevate himself above his colleagues. While that's all well and good, he is simply one person. The government should bring in expatriates to teach local physicians, thereby increasing the number of doctors with expertise in a variety of areas.

There is also a need to examine how the system can allow doctors to go on perpetual strike, when their oath is to discharge their duties to save lives. Given the nature of the care they provide, it is unclear whether that oath includes the tenet "do no harm."

It is also imperative that the government examine how nurses are trained, so they can provide more sophisticated care in the absence of doctors who are either in short supply or can walk out on a moment's notice. Nurse practitioners should be required to work in hospitals to learn roles that doctors may not be available to take on. This strategy is very successful in the United States, and more so where doctors are in short supply. For their part, doctors cannot be threatened by the emergence of this new cadre of health care workers. It is all for the good of the country.

Without such training, there will always be a chasm in delivery of quality and timely health care to the populace. In my view, it is utterly unconscionable that key institutions and government entities can stand by while its vulnerable masses, the soul of the nation, perish.

The World Health Organization (WHO) reports Nigeria's physician-to-patient ratio is 4 doctors per 10,000 patients. Data from WorldAtlas shows that Qatar, which ranks number one, and Cuba, number three, report figures that are much higher, 77.4 per 10,000 and 62.7 per 10,000, respectively. Many factors contribute to these figures, but shortages remain. The need for nurses to assume more important roles in the health care system becomes paramount given the brain drain of doctors that is endemic in the country.

Many experts, including doctors, have written about the flawed system of health care in this resource-rich nation. We simply add our voices to theirs for a collective echo in the halls of power.

I returned home with my siblings who also lived in the United States to bury our beloved Sally. Oluchi, now nine, accompanied us as well. Explaining her mother's death, and why she looked like she did right before she died, was no easy feat. Our little gift from Sally was reluctant to say that was even her mother. Although her body had fed on itself, and she had been racked with pain, the true Sally remains a treasure in our hearts.

We are saddened by our loss, but we just know her death will not be in vain. The system of care in this rich country is broken, and more needs to be done if there's ever going to be any advancement in the field of medicine and in life expectancy among its citizens. Many there die young, and there is no end in sight. Nigeria, the eyes of the Lord are upon you. May the Almighty God intervene, in His divine mercy, to raise the consciousness of the people who can drive your advancement. God bless Nigeria!

To the village doctor who has spent most of his adult life in a village far away from his urban dwelling and who left his own state to be a beacon of life to total strangers, we say thank you. While your facility is far from being a state-of-the-art hospital, you managed to offer the less fortunate among us a place to go for basic care. I remember you treating an aunt whose leg had been mauled by a dog owned by one of her husband's kin and who almost lost the leg to gangrene, because she could not afford the 2,000 Naira ($10 USD) to pay for her care. My phone call to you resolved all that. Her leg was taken care of with a series of injections and careful wound care by nurses who are devoted to the care of their patients. It is rumored that you will be leaving the village hospital and returning to private life, and the villagers' sense of fear and abandonment is already palpable. However, there's a new hospital opening near the market square. God, take control!

I am a proponent of every one of us lifting up one or two others. Therefore, we must all help reshape the nature of health care in Nigeria. My plea is that, as we each struggle to make sense of our own lives, we are not so focused on our own problems that we overlook our God-given purpose to help others. Because there's someone out there whose destiny is tied to ours, and who is rooting for us to survive and thrive. We are each our brother's keeper. Whatever you can contribute to help change the lives of others, just do it! To that doctor who loved Sally, you know who you are. Thank you.

It is always darkest just before the day dawneth.

—Thomas Fuller, 1650

ACKNOWLEDGMENTS

To my mother, Abigail, to whom the loss of a daughter remains an unimaginable pain. We understand still that this pain relays a silent tug of inexplicable joy on your grateful heart. We, too, are grateful for your unflinching strength and divine wisdom. You are a woman of substance. Your children are aware that God's gift of Sally to you represents the best of us (she was our anointed watchman).

To the special daughter of Salome, Oluchi, you were the pride and joy of your mother. She had you against all odds, a true miracle. Did you know that she would stare at you, smile, and then she would lovingly call out your name, "Oluchi"? As if with pride, she was saying, "Is this real, did little me do this?" She was in awe of the awesomeness of God, which is represented in you. May you fulfill your destiny to the praise of Yahweh, in honor of your mother's memory.

To my sister Adanne, who never stopped giving of herself to ensure our entire family's progress, and through whom Sally enjoyed a little part of life: we all treasure you. And to my sister

Ra, who, with a broken heart, travailed the Nigerian broken health care system with me: you are greatly appreciated.

My husband, Segun, your generosity of heart is matched only by your ability to provide a shoulder for all to lean on. Your compassion and divine wisdom will never go unrewarded by God Almighty. Cousin Ndi, the glue given to us by Adonai that held us together during those daunting, dark days as we traveled through the maze of the health care system, and Chinedu and our brother-in-law Remi, thank you.

To my siblings (Dorcas, Christy, Di, Kem, and Chidi), who loved Sally so dearly, who contributed ideas, emotional support, funds, and prayers, and who received the saddest news of their lives, the loss of a beloved sister, we remain grateful to our Lord Jesus Christ, who remains forever loving.

And to my longtime special friend Gary Frisch, your support, encouragement, and editorial assistance remain greatly appreciated.

To my good friend, God's blessed warrior, Marion Yartey, remain forever blessed by God. Dua Kobenan Jean Luc Kra "Papa Jean," God's servant, the family appreciates your love and spiritual support. Thank you, Man of God Nana Bentil, for blessing us with your divine instructions and guidance. I am better for knowing your love for God.

ABOUT THIS BOOK

Wounded Hearts: My Roller-Coaster Journey into Third-World Health Care traces my journey through Nigeria's broken health care system after my annual trip to visit family there was interrupted by the illness of my younger sister, Sally. The unexpected loss of this laughter-filled young woman with disability, who died a senseless death at the hands of a poorly trained surgeon, inspired this narrative, which sadly only hints at the inadequacy of a system designed to treat the nation's estimated 206 million people.

I was compelled to detail this journey, with all its horrible twists and turns, to both raise awareness in the rest of the world and as a call to action for a new generation of Nigerians and their leaders to pick up the mantle and effect change.

Within this story, I also detail the birth of this special sister, God's grace upon her life, an unexpected pregnancy, and the miraculous birth of her only child. Thus, this book offers readers first-hand insight into sisterly love and the pain of losing a loved one.

The competing needs of doctors to either survive or care for their patients often leaves the citizens at a disadvantage. Perhaps a day is coming when our better angels will replace greed, and a thriving health care system will emerge. Hopefully, you will be drawn into the belly of this flawed system of care or, better yet, add your voice to the rising crescendo for the urgent need for Nigeria to invest in itself and its people.

ABOUT THE AUTHOR

As a socio-medical researcher, Dr. Patience Akinosho shares her story from her experiences and encounters with some cogs of Africa's failing health care system. She received her Bachelor of Science degree from Kean University and holds a Master of Science degree from Rutgers University School of Public Administration. She also received her master of public health in socio-medical sciences and her doctorate from the Mailman School of Public Health at Columbia University and was the recipient of a dissertation fellowship from the International Development Research Center in Canada. Her commitment to the causes of the forgotten, particularly women, children, and the elderly, has led her to initiate and direct several public health and microfinance initiatives in Nigeria, helping to raise the health and economic standards of disenfranchised populations. Guided by her Christian beliefs, Dr. Akinosho has helped many villages in Nigeria obtain health care by sponsoring and cosponsoring free mobile medical care services in collaboration with expatriates now living in the United States, local physicians, nurses, and pharmacists.